PAPER CLAY

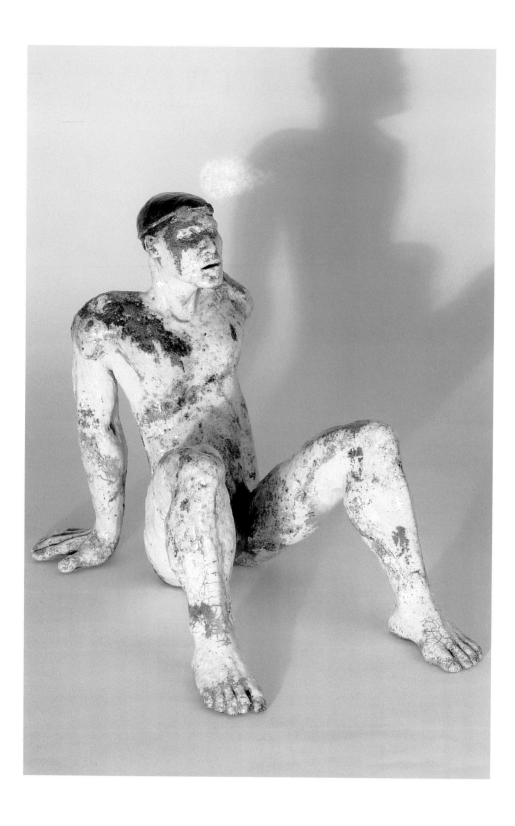

PAPER CLAY

Rosette Gault

A&C Black • London

University of Pennsylvania Press • Philadelphia

First published in Great Britain in 2005
A & C Black Publishers Limited
Alderman House, 37 Soho Square
London W1D 3QZ
www.acblack.com

ISBN 07136-6827-X

Published simultaneously in the USA by
University of Pennsylvania Press
4200 Pine Street
Philadelphia, Pennsylvania 19104-4011

ISBN 0-8122-1895-7

Book design by Susan McIntyre.
Cover design by Sutchinda Rangsi Thompson.

COVER IMAGE (FRONT): *Social Face*, figure by Leslie Lee
(USA). Earthenware, height: 45 cm (17 ¾ in.).
COVER IMAGE (BACK): Book by Nancy Selvin (USA).
FRONTISPIECE: Raku figure by Carmen Lang.
CONTENTS PAGE: *Red Spiral* by Ed Bamiling (Canada).

Printed and bound in Singapore by Tien Wah
Press Ltd

A & C Black uses paper produced with elemental
chlorine-free pulp, harvested from managed
sustainable forests.

Contents

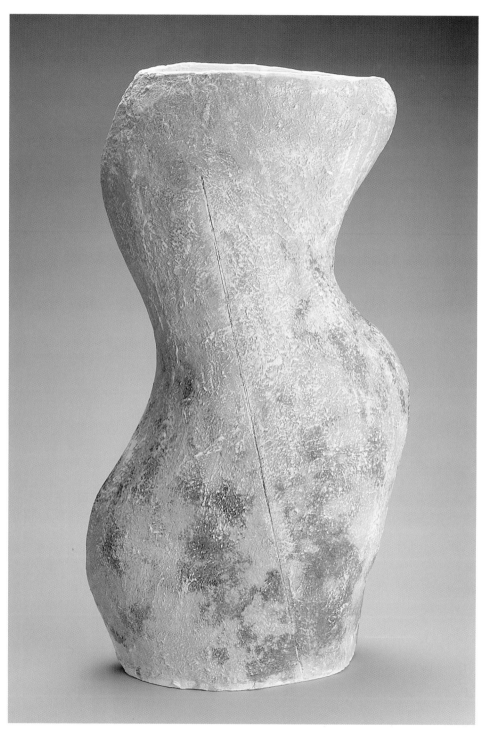

Scandinavian Influence by Rosette Gault (USA), 81 × 35.5 cm (32 × 14 in.).

History and Overview

This is a book about clay and it's a book about freedom. It's also a book about a discovery. It's about imagination unbounded and a practical means to bring fresh vision to the ceramic form. It's about a familiar ceramic material for kilns even more versatile than previously believed.

What forms of imagination in ceramic art do we see nowadays that would have been impossible or impractical to achieve in the past? Some answers to this question will be found in this book, and more will be forthcoming no doubt.

As you can imagine, the use of paper clay has now spread through many countries via teacher/student and colleague networks so that it now seems that 'experts' can appear at every turn. Many teachers now include paper clay and I am very happy that understanding and good uses for this form of clay are being developed, so I give thanks to all the students and their questions and to the people behind the scenes who support this work. It is due to this enthusiasm for paper clay that greater clarity of information is available today than at the time of writing the first edition.

Highlights and overview

What paper clay is

Paper clay is, as the name suggests, a half solid, half fluid plastic modelling mix of clay, paper pulp and water. The proportion of clay in the mix is greater than the proportion of paper, so objects constructed in this material can be fired intact in kilns without turning to dust as the paper burns off. Furthermore, the paper pulp that we add to the clay can be easily made from recycled office papers or newspapers in the artist's studio.

Unique features and freedoms

Extremely strong as greenware, paper clay can be worked in multiple layers of wet over dry, and altered at nearly any stage in the forming process. The final glazed and fired result can be indistinguishable from conventional clay. Some of the sculptural freedoms shown here have never been possible with conventional clays. Some paper clays have also been found to be frost-proof.

Paper clay is also of practical help for the busy teacher as firing work becomes a choice, not a necessity. If time to fire 'disappears', or if a kiln is not available, give the works a quick coat of seal such as white glue and water mixed 50/50 to set the surface. The works can be stained and sponged to show off textures in a jiffy. Acrylic paint, nail polish, or buffed up car-wax are finishes that might suit teachers.

Impact on the ceramics tradition

Paper clay handles both like and unlike the clay and paper it is made of. Paper clay has its own unique characteristics. This book will enable you, the maker, the creator, to understand how this is so, from the ground up, so to speak. The ceramicist's view serves as a point of departure for a much broader perspective in the field of art. Whether you are an artist, potter, sculptor, scientist, beginner or professional, the contents of this book should assist you in making an informed decision about paper clay.

Technical developments

Clay tradition

Pottery clay has earned a love/hate reputation among sculptors. Though seductive because it is malleable at first touch, the truth is that the process of making from that point on can be a challenge. If the pottery clay dries out

unevenly and cracks, the work is beyond repair. Even if the form dries intact, it will often be fragile. Safe transport at this stage, whether to the kiln or to a new shelf, can be worrisome. Clay needs firing in kilns. Glazes are yet another skill to learn. Fraught with potential failures, the pottery process requires time and persistence to master. It is not a medium for the faint of heart or the inexperienced.

Ceramic science teaches that to stop cracks an ideal additive to a clay would have to be some material that stops clay from shrinking as it dries. When my first tests of paper clay in the 1970s shrank, I assumed they had failed. If pulp in clay did not solve the shrinkage, it would be impossible for it to solve the cracks. The idea that clay for firing could ever be worked wet over dry was totally beyond my conception of reality at that time.

Most clay makers, in the past, disqualified paper pulp from serious consideration as a viable ceramic filler. Cellulose, the main ingredient in paper pulp, is primarily an organic carbon compound[1] combustible in fire. The reasoning was: why bother to add it at all? Paper makers, meanwhile, have long known that small proportions of clay are good 'filler' for paper recipes because clay fills in and smoothes out pockets in the fibrous texture of paper.

Paper technology

Today's paper pulp is one of several key 'high tech' innovations which had to happen *before* its use in contemporary paper clay could be developed to the current state. For example, ways to make papers from wood have been found relatively recently, i.e. within the past two hundred years.

Figure by Eliisa Isoniemi (Finland).

RIGHT *Future Book* by Rosette Gault (USA). *Photograph courtesy of Banff Centre (Don Lee).*

Until 25 years ago the personal computer was unknown and copy machines were in their infancy. Today, these machines generate printed paper in quantity. Also, the recent invention of the scanning electron microscope has made the inner workings and structure of clays and minerals visible for the first time.

As for clay body fillers, there were already many choices, as we shall see in the next chapter. What features were noticed about pulp, such as the short shelf life or loss of fired strength, were, more often than not, considered liabilities.

It was not until 1990 that I pursued this subject further. During my artist

BELOW *Emerging Angel* by Rosette Gault (USA). *Photograph by Roger Schreiber.*

residency at the Banff Centre in Canada a few of us artist residents[2] had tried various recipes of paper clay and used it just as if it were a conventional clay for coils, slab construction, 'paper'-like sheets, and even the wheel. Of course it worked for us, we never thought for a moment that it wouldn't. None of us realised fully how close we were to a discovery.

Blooming Bureaucracy by Graham Hay (Australia), 59 × 46 × 46 cm (23¼ × 18 × 18 in.).

A spirit of playfulness and experimentation led me to try the very unorthodox method of healing a huge crack in a bone dry paper clay sculpture. I had nothing to lose, because the loss, i.e. crack, would be guaranteed, or so I thought. Much to my surprise, the crack was healed. My first guess recipe turned out to be good enough. I pursued the idea further.
I tested the limits of paper clay again and again for my sculptural work. Eventually I came to understand the expanded sculptural possibility for paper clays was a reliable fact. I presented the concept formally to colleagues at a 1992 ceramics conference in Helsinki, Finland. The same year my first article on the subject was published. Five years later, the information had spread worldwide and a book such as this could be written. I am thankful for the support of a vast international network of people who have contributed to this project along the way.

In this new edition, professional artists and advanced students who desire to make large-scale sculpture of high-fired porcelain, terracotta or earthenware paper clay now have access to more comprehensive information that specifically clarifies, refines and sums up construction and/or carving methods that stand up to repeated firing tests. Sand-cast methods partner large-scale so well that additional guidance specific to paper/plaster is here too. Also included are more recipes for large-scale sculptural works in case you wish to mix your own clay.

Historical context of the discovery

Long history of fibres and clay mixtures

Contemporary paper clay is descended from several well-established bodies of knowledge and tradition. Each branch of paper clay relatives has its own unique history and features. For starters, there are both fired and unfired forms of paper clay. Various mixtures and forms of paper clay have been known to us for centuries. The differences between paper clays often overlap, as you will see. But it will be helpful to clarify what we can. Adobe is a common and ancient building material used in places where the geography, climate and soil permit. Unfired building bricks of clay and straw, 'adobe', are surprisingly strong even unfired. In spite of the enormous difference in magnitude between adobe and paper clays, I like to think of paper clay as a form of 'high tech adobe' because paper fibres and straw share a similar hollow, flexible tube shape.

In India, unfired forms of papier maché clay have a history that stretches thousands of years. Everything from aromatic spices, mashed rags, paper, grass, cow dung and mango leaves to iron filings, sand, rice hull and bamboo has been added to clays in India depending on what the clay was going to be used for. There is a form of papier maché clay for unfired use, a casting moulding clay of 40 parts clay, 50 paper and 10 tree gum[3] (which is called Kagazi Kumba). Another recipe, called Kari Kbumba, is 70 parts clay, 20 paper and 10 tree gum. These are used in theatres and art centres like clay maché. In India, these unfired clays are used for religious icons and ritual objects that can be handled easily. Sometimes these forms were intended to be impermanent. At the final stage of some rituals, large-scale icons and effigies are immersed in river waters to the point of dissolution.

Also included in the 'not for firing in kilns' category of paper clay mixtures are the extensive array of air-set building and art materials. Papier maché-based clays exist with colours, glues and/ or hardeners[4] added. Flour and water mix well for modelling too. Though flour is not technically a paper, it does contain cellulose. Most children's 'paper' clays with glues in them harden in the air and would crumble to dust if fired in a kiln. Some polymer plastic clays (e.g. Fimo or Sculpti) are yet further variations on the same idea. For hardeners in non-fired paper clays, plaster of Paris, glues or lignins (a cellulose by-product) are often used.

Tool Box by Victor Spinski (USA). *The box is press-moulded using 15% (by volume) pulp and cast objects, using 10% pulp. I had to get this project done in a week, so the paper clay came to my rescue. No signs of fast firing problems either.*

clay is not actually mentioned as part of this recipe[6]. The spicy aroma that lasts long after the material or 'rag mud' has dried was called 'an extraordinary sense experience' by those involved. Also during the same project, Rauschenberg was reported as having to abandon a sculpture in progress which was made of some kind of pulp or rag and clay mix because of its smell, and because it attracted insects in the high heat and humidity.

In Sèvres, France, Jean-Pierre Béranger devised a means of making translucent porcelain paper clay paper sheets which could then be folded, wrapped or printed on. His 1987 method was very similar to the papermaking process.[7] He noticed

History of 'paper clay' sheets

Paper clay has long been formed into flat paper-like sheets, versions of which have been reported in India, Japan, France, Australia, the USA and other countries since the 1950s or before. As far as is documented, industrial and artistic uses for the two-dimensional products include fired ceramic 'paper' to be hung on a wall, tiles of all sizes and even liners for kiln shelves.

Robert Rauschenberg[5], when in India for the Gemini-India Project in May 1975, used a local material called 'rag mud'. This was a mixture of paper pulp, fenugreek powder, ground tamarind seed, copper sulphate, and water. Silk from saris and ropes and strings were incorporated in the pulp as it was set up flat in a wood frame screen such as those used by paper makers. As you can see,

RIGHT *Social Face*, figure by Leslie Lee (USA). Earthenware, height: 45 cm (17¾ in.).

Like Father, Like Son by Dan Keegan (USA), 81 × 36 × 20 cm (32 × 14¼ × 8 in.).

sheets were purchased almost leather-hard, encased in plastic. The plastic was peeled off before use and firing. The paper clay could be trimmed with scissors. A multitude of origami and folded paper structures could be made using the conventional methods. These products were known in the US in the craft and toy stores by the early 1980s. Paper companies in Japan and elsewhere also did extensive research to develop other classes of paper, using synthetic fibres, fibreglass and nylons with pulp.

Meanwhile, since the 1970s (or possibly earlier), the making of flat sheets of pulp clay has been in progress on nearly every continent, though certainly the use has been sporadic and not common. Its use was spread through exchange visits by artists and conversations with ceramic engineers. An exact origin is difficult to trace because the idea of mixing pulp in clay has such a long and variegated history. If sculptural paper clay for firing was known, it was never considered remarkable enough to write about. To my knowledge most, if not all, of these artists related to 'paper' clay as if it were a ceramic paper for printing or painting with glaze or other colours. Many people did experiments, and some of them were sculptural experiments with paper clay. However, more often than not, the projects were abandoned because the paper clay started to smell or perhaps because a more complete understanding of this medium was needed.

that the shrinkage of porcelain clays and paper pulps were very similar and found that the paper porcelain sheets were versatile to handle and translucent to fire. He reported that traces of pulp ash cause a slight colour change in porcelains. This has been confirmed in recent research also. He also travelled to Japan and there was much exchange about these methods at that time.

The Japanese found a means of screening flat sheets of coloured paper clays. Coloured 'paper' clay could be cut into shapes with a knife before application, assembly and firing. The A4 size

Nowhere No. 2 by Leslie Lee (USA), length: 40 cm (15¾ in.).

Notes

1. Cellulose contains traces of inorganic minerals bonded in the lignins. At high temperatures the trace of ash can be a flux in some clays.
2. Ibrahim Wagh, Alec Sorotoschysnki, Denise Buckley and Jennifer Clark, but others were at Banff too who have since adopted the medium. Ed Bamiling and Les Manning were also present. Their vision to bring an international group of artists together for a work period was catalytic.
3. Tree gum: a naturally occurring resin, source of high lignin, functions as a hardener.
4. Celluclay™ has plaster as the hardener. Celluclay™ is not for firing in kilns.
5. Kenneth Tyler and Rosamund Felson, 'Two Rauschenberg Paper Projects' in *Paper, Art & and Technology*, ed. Paulette Long, World Print Council, 1979.
6. Gemini-India Project, 1951–1953.
7. Photos of this process are found in *La Revue de la Ceramique et du Verre*, no. 34, Mai Juin 1987, 'Papier Porcelaine' by Francoise Espagnet (article in French).

Chapter One

Clay Ingredients and Additives

Even if you ultimately never prepare your own clay or even paper clay, the more you understand about clay bodies and their components, the more control you have over the fired result. Paper clay ceramic could not exist without an existing foundation knowledge of compatible clay and glaze chemistry. In this sense, paper clay is an offshoot of ceramic science. As such I call the science of paper clay a 'second generation' ceramics. Since all clays are potential candidates for conversion to paper clay, some of the key facts regarding ceramic clays and the extra ingredients commonly used in recipes are reviewed here.

Clays

Clay in and of itself is a dry powder. Potters' clays are really clay and water combinations. Clays are composed of a wide variety of alumina silicate minerals based on the rocks found in a specific geographic region. In each location the composition of the clay will be unique to that area of the world.

LEFT Stoneware vessel by Birgit Krogh (Denmark).

RIGHT Scanning electron micrograph (SEM) of kaolin clay particles, some as small as 0.2 microns in length.
Photograph courtesy of Walter Keller.

Composition/sources

Earthenware, terracotta, raku, china ware, stoneware and porcelain are some of the most common terms used throughout the world to describe families of clays with similar characteristics of either melting point, colour, particle size or appearance. More specific information about these clay groups will come in the next chapter. The majority of compatible ceramic glazes that match these clays are composed in whole or in part of the same minerals as the clays, but in different proportions.

Particles

Clay particles are among the smallest that are found in nature. Kaolins have been measured to be from 0.1 micron up to 10 microns or more. The average size is between 0.2–0.4 microns in length. Potters distinguish, by feel if not by eye,

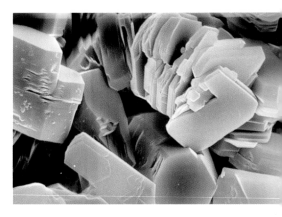

the clays with the tiniest and flattest clay particles such as kaolins or ball clays from the more coarse fireclays and stonewares. The particle size and shape can make a difference in the handling and firing properties. Most studio clays today contain a variety of particle shapes and/or sizes from various deposits around the world.

Clay slip

Liquid watered-down clay can be mixed in all varieties and concentrations from thin to thick and paste-like. It is a fabulous adhesive for clay and it has 1001 other uses for sculptors – for surface treatments, texture and colour. It can be brushed, sponged, dipped and even sprayed. It is easy to make, and the recipes are highly compatible and interchangeable with a wide variety of clays.

Paper clay slips, which I call p'slip, can also be made. P'slip is superb for use as an all-purpose ceramic adhesive, no matter whether the clay you join does or does not contain paper. Also, p'slips may be applied as surface treatments and textures.

Water as an additive

Adjustments to the water used in clay such as electrolytes, wetting agents and soluble minerals have a variety of purposes, especially in slips, but also in clay and glazes. In clay and glaze, solubility of the clay minerals in water can affect the working properties. For example, free floating clay particles in tap water

LEFT *Standing House* by Nina Hole (Denmark), height: 50 cm (19¾ in.).

RIGHT *Silence at the Desk Top*, by Rosette Gault (USA), 30 × 7 × 12 cm (11¾ × 2¾ × 4¾ in.), screened glazes, then carved.

A cup by Pottery Northwest (USA) participant. Pinched cup and cast handle, assembled at dry stage.

based slips group together and settle to the bottom of the bucket within several hours. For a casting slip to pour well, a dense and uniform fluid suspension of clay particles is best. To achieve this effect, 'deflocculent' or 'electrolyte' chemicals can be added to the water to change the electrical chemistry of the water so that clay particles nest more tightly with one another but have less friction to one another. The particles will then flow easily and the ultra dense clay fluid will pour in long, smooth ribbons. Electrolytes such as sodium silicate/soda ash or Darvan are the most common additives for casting slips. However not all ceramic minerals and clays respond to the dispersal chemicals in the water the same way. Only some clays can be converted into casting slips.[1] All casting slips can be converted to paper clays or paper clay slips. Wetting agents such as Orzan[2] can be useful, particularly in ultra-high grog inert non-shrink clay bodies.

Common Additives and Clay Fillers

Ground bricks (grog/chamotte)

Chamotte or grog is already biscuit or mature fired bricks/fireclays which have been mechanically ground and meshed to a variety of irregular granular shapes and sizes from coarse (like rough grit) to fine powder. Because most grog is immature (partially fired biscuit) clay, it is water-absorbent in a clay body, and it is not compressible. The water absorbency of chamotte helps mitigate some drying problems in conventional clay.

Chamotte corrects and compensates for many clay faults, though not as many as pulp does. This non-plastic additive is a popular way to provide both fired texture and 'tooth' to clays. Grog is of neutral shrinkage in clays at room or bisque temperatures. Earthenware grogs from red bricks may be mature at the bisque temperature range and could melt to glassy glaze nips in high-fired stoneware clays.

Before paper clay was known, most large-scale works were impossible without grog of some kind. After firing, most chamotte leaves a telltale gritty surface texture and is tan to rust in colour. Grog is usually purchased dry in 20 kg (44 lb) bags. It is either wedged into clays by hand, or added directly to the dry mix in clay-making machines. Molochite, a refractory porcelain grog, may be used for whiteware. A small to modest amount of grog in a paper clay is acceptable where surface texture is desired.

Silica sand

Sand or SiO_2 also comes in a wide variety of granulation from fine to coarse. Silica is the most commonly used non-clay 'filler'. However, its use must be considered carefully, because it can have a number of effects. Its presence can affect and possibly improve glaze fit, especially at the stoneware and porcelain temperatures. Many people like its sandy texture. At the high temperatures, for example, coarse sand may even partially melt into tiny glass bits visible on unglazed surfaces. Occasionally, however, coarse mesh silica sand has impurities (i.e. bits of other minerals) which can cause discolouration, bloating and other problems.

Group of figures by Ann Verdacourt (New Zealand), height: 25.5 cm (10 in.).

Sand, like grog, is usually purchased in 20 kg (44 lb) bags with different mesh granulations. It is either wedged into clays by hand, or added directly to the dry mix in clay-making machines. If there is silica flour in the base recipe, you can replace some of the silica flour with granulated silica for more texture. Silica-flour bearing clay formulae are normally not affected by adding cellulose.

Fibreglass (silica)

Another form of silica is fibreglass: a technological wonder. Fibreglass is spun silica, literally glass strands. If you find source of fluff fibreglass, this can be incorporated into the clay body for fibre strength both before and after the firing. These fibres are less flexible than nylon however. The fibres are not hollow and resist water compared to cellulose. Fibreglass, in high-fired clays, fuses inside the clay body like the glass it is. At high-fire temperatures some woven fibreglass fires translucent when placed on a small window frame of refractory opaque clay. Its use as a reinforcement in high-fire ceramics was suggested in the US by the late Daniel Rhodes: 'Saturate the woven fibreglass patches as much as possible in slip. Apply the patches or strips over leatherhard seams to reinforce the interiors of large-scale forms.'[3]

Sawdust

Sawdust is an unrefined form of cellulose which is not yet sufficiently processed to the scale of individual fibres. It is commonly used in clays for bricks and many sculptures. When sawdust burns away during the firing, a variety of tiny air pockets are visible and the result is a soft/light brick or sculpture with a pocked surface texture. The relative size of the average sawdust granule next to a paper pulp cellulose fibre is enormous, something like comparing a giant rock boulder to a strand of hair. As a filler, sawdust voids open up a clay body and therefore heat travels through the mass more easily. The more sawdust in the recipe, the less plastic the clay body will be. Also, sawdust is hydrophilic and may retard the drying process. In smaller amounts, it gives a relatively mild improvement in green strength. I think of sawdust as a giant tangled knot of crimped up cellulose fibres that are only 25% functional compared to what they could be were they processed pulp. The sawdust particles swell slightly with water. Compared to grog, sawdust will compress slightly during the clay shrinkage process.

Sawdust and pulp can work well in combination. Sawdust is usually found near wood shops and most potters or sculptors can bag it up themselves. It can be either wedged into clays by hand, or added directly to the dry mix in clay-making machines. Sawdust has many other uses in the clay studio, not least as a fuel for kilns. Store sawdust carefully and avoid open flames as airborne sawdust can be surprisingly volatile.

Vermiculite

Vermiculite is an alumina silicate mineral compound in the mica (montmorillonite) family used as an additive in garden soils for drainage (see Appendix for picture). It is also used for thermal insulation products and building materials. The coarse, variegated pellet has been expanded or fluffed up in a kiln, and flat chips break off the pellet easily. Granulated chunks of vermiculite appear in a variety of mesh sizes. It is very water absorbent up to 500°C (932°F) but after 700°C (1292°F)

Chair by Betty Engleholm (Denmark).

it will not rehydrate. For larger-scale works, it is often added to reduce the fired weight, because it, like pulp, burns away leaving a trace of mineral ash. Vermiculite usually leaves visible pock marks and open pores on the fired clay surface.

It, too, can be used in conjunction with pulp in a clay body if a surface texture is desired. However, as with many other additives, if you add high proportions of vermiculite, you may get less than desirable results. The loss of plasticity will be dramatic. Like sawdust, vermiculite will retard the drying in your clay body.

Perlite

Perlite is a volcanic silica-based additive to clays that comes in two sizes: the larger pellet for horticulture and a smaller grain for use with plaster compounds and insulation building materials. It is used to open up the clay body and it makes raku firing of non-paper bearing fireclay recipes much easier. Perlite in the clay is water absorbent. Perlite, like vermiculite, has been heat processed. Under a scanning electron micrograph this 'pseudo-popcorn' looks like a cluster of tiny mineral bubbles. After firing to cone 8, perlite shrinks back to its non-'popcorn' size leaving a trace of mica in the void. For example, one could mix a rough sculpture body using about 20–25% perlite by volume of dry fireclay with about 2–5% grog (for strength).[4] It should be carved only at leatherhard. It is brittle at 1250°C (2282°F) so refires at cone 10 are risky. It is suitable for single firings that skip the bisque stage. It is possible to raku fire work raw with high perlite bodies (see Appendix for recipe).

Special purpose additives

Kyanite is an ultra-refractory clay (alumina silicate) from a mine in Virginia, USA, which forms mullite crystals easily at high temperatures. Kyanite dramatically improves the fired strength of low-fired sculptural work (see Appendix for recipe). Victor Spinski reports that paper clay bodies with kyanite are nearly indestructible. In some high-fired clays the proportion should be reduced to 5% however.[5]

Bentonites are unique clay (alumina silicate) minerals of extremely tiny colloidal particles[6] that, when mixed with water, radically expand to make a gelatine-like goo or thick paste. This tends to help plasticise otherwise short clay. The trouble is that after the water evaporates in the mix, the bentonite size shrinks 30% back to normal when it dries. Thus, cracking would be expected on non-paper clays with too much bentonite. (The maximum recommended for a plasticiser in glaze is 2% of the dry weight.[7] In high additive clay body formulae or porcelains, do not exceed 6%.[8])

For clay bodies which can withstand drastic thermal shock or direct flame, lithium-based feldspars, like spodumene and petalite, are often found in the base recipe. Paper clays may be converted from lithium-based recipes if the general guidelines for additives are followed.

Wollastonite and the calcium group

Wollastonite (a calcium silicate) is two additives in one. In a clay recipe, it helps reduce shrinkage, improves fired hardness and is a source of silica for the high-temperature clays (see Appendix). Paper clays with wollastonite will respond well in firing. Other forms of calcium are plaster and cement. Such mixtures with clay are rarely fired. Strict testing of clays with plaster is necessary to avoid possible rehydration and expansion (read miniature explosion) that creates holes in the fired clay days, weeks, months or years later.

Colourants and texturisers

To get coloured specks and pocks in clay bodies, impurities such as the granular metallic oxides, manganese, rutile, ilmenite, auto valve grindings, metal file shavings, nails or wire fragments of copper and steel scrubbing pads can be introduced. For unusual textures, artists have used anything combustible such as rice, lentils, chopped grass, dehydrated pet food, cat litter pellets, pasta, coffee grinds, string, Styrofoam pellets, nut shells and even garden dirt.

Nylon

Nylon is a man-made fibre which has been used in clay bodies as a fibre source for sculptural forms when soft clay sheets were to be draped and folded to mimic fabric cloth and leather. Its chief benefit, compared to cellulose and when used in a moist clay recipe, is a longer shelf life. The presence of either nylon or cellulose increases the green strength of clays dramatically.

Nylon fibres are smooth miniature extrusions. Chemical (A) is extruded through a 'spinneret' device that resembles a miniature shower nozzle. During the extrusion, the spinneret is immersed in a chemical solution (B). Chemical A reacts with Chemical B under the right conditions of temperature, pressure, motion and viscosity to produce strands of nylon 'fibre'. The strands are then chopped off at the desired lengths.

Nylon is not hollow; it is barely water absorbent. Depending upon the chemistry, nylon may be stretchy in one or two directions only. Nylon fibres do not compress well and are nearly impossible to carve. Most nylon fibres for clay bodies are three to 100 times longer in length than the average paper fibre. Wedging and cutting through a block of moist nylon clay with a wire produces a lot of drag. Because nylon fibres clog most clay-mixing equipment, nylon has to be wedged into the clay by hand.

Paper clays with nylon fibres are popular with some artists. Perhaps these artists require less wet over dry capability and they have a technique with the nylon already established. If you use both nylon and cellulose, keep an eye on the total ratio of plastic clay to non-clay additives. Adding too much of either fibre could seriously affect your results.

Cellulose

Cellulose fibre is the primary natural ingredient found in most paper and as a clay body additive, it has distinct characteristics. These are discussed in detail in the next chapter.

Notes

1 Small-particle clays work best with dispersal agents (courtesy of Fabens, Notkin and Keyes).
2 Orzan is a trade name for a pulp industry cellulose byproduct: sodium lignosulfate. As a wetting agent and adhesive plasticiser, it has a high chemical affinity for silica and other unfired mineral compounds. (It can make even sand castles nearly rock hard.) According to Jerry Rothman, it is nontoxic, and the powder is readily soluble in water before use.
3 Daniel Rhodes quoted at Pottery Northwest Workshop, Seattle, 1985.
4 John McCuiston's sculpture recipe is a large scoop of grog, a full 5 gallon bucketful of perlite, and about 80 lb of Lincoln fireclay to about 4 gallons of water.
5 Victor Spinski; University of Delaware (see p. 36).
6 Colloidal particles are 0.03% the size of the average kaolinite particle; some are smaller than can be measured with visible light (Fournier). Bentonite is thought to be airborne volcanic dust (Chappell).
7 Calcium bentonite swells less than the sodium bentonites (Fournier).
8 A more expensive substitute for bentonite is Macaloid which does not shrink so much (for more information see Peterson, in Bibliography).

Chapter Two

Paper and Paper Clay Preparation

Description

When viewed under a microscope, paper appears as a network of compressed tubular cellulose fibres. When paper scraps are stirred vigorously in a soup of hot water, paper will break down to soft wet pulp and the cellulose fibres will separate. In this condition it can be stored or added to clays.

Cellulose fibre is a remarkable multipurpose additive to clays. Most ceramicists are unfamiliar with cellulose so a closer look at it will be useful here.

Cellulose fibres and lignin

The molecular structure of each cellulose tube appears as an intricate and sturdy coil. Chain patterns of carbon

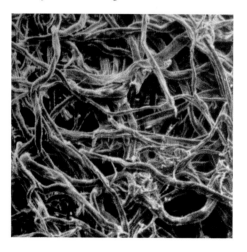

and hydrogen spiral around the hollow centre called the lumen. There are two classes of cellulose in paper recipes: cellulose proper (C_6H_{12}) and hemi-cellulose ($C_{12}H_{22}$). As you might guess from the molecular label, hemi-cellulose is almost double the size and complexity as a compound of plain cellulose. Cellulose is hydrophilic: it absorbs water.

The coating on the exterior of each tube of cellulose is a layer of lignin that could be thick or thin depending on the plant source. Lignin behaves like a hydrophobic, or water repellent, compound.[1] Therefore, water at one end of the straw of cellulose can be wicked up the interior of the hollow tube with minimum evaporation. Lignin chemicals bond with a variety of inorganic minerals.[2] Depending on the species, lignin compound structures contain various amounts of minerals which accumulate as the plant or tree grows. The minerals lend strength by leaching up the plant via water osmosis from the soil. Tree wood and bark cellulose contain many more minerals and, correspondingly, more lignin than flax, linen or cotton. Wood pulp is normally 25–30% lignin, and cellulose from cotton is about 2% lignin.

Scanning electron micrograph (SEM) close-up of paper fibre.
Photograph courtesy of Roy Whitney.

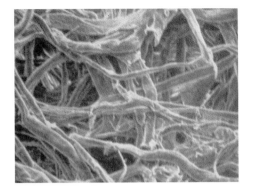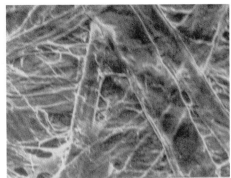
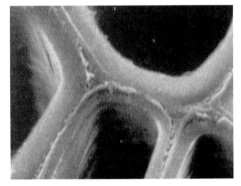

Scanning Electron Micrographs (SEMs) of papers. Tubular and hollow fibres are normal in top left, but flatten under high compression (top right), and medium compression (bottom left).

Cross section of a hardwood fibre (lower right) shows cellulose tissue, lumen (black hollow area) and lignin (white adhesive seal). *Photographs courtesy of Roy Whitney.*

The cellulose structural system offers an efficient, flexible and resilient means of moving water through the earth. Water is both conserved and directed to where the need is greatest.

Paper fibres are analysed to determine how much and what kind of cellulose they contain, and how much lignin is present. Paper-makers avoid high lignin cellulose because the acidic lignin, in time, turns papers yellow as it oxidises. Newsprint is a good example of a high lignin paper. Cotton, linen, and flax based cellulose sources have less lignin, and tend to go yellow more slowly. Pure rag archival papers (100%), prized by paper-makers, tend not to yellow at room temperature because they have minimum lignin. For ceramics, the paper, lignins and inks ultimately burn away in the fire. Unlike the paper-maker, the ceramicist has no long-term concern about lignin.

Cellulose, whether derived from cotton linter or wood pulp, leaves a trace of ash when fired on its own. At cone 8 however, some forms of cellulose melt to a small glassy residue.

Another feature which paper-makers prize is fibre length. Longer fibres for a paper-maker mean the handmade paper will knit together nicely and not tear easily. But for the ceramicist, the longer fibre length is actually not the most useful. My experience is that the long fibres in clay give noticeably more green strength but are more difficult to pull a cutting wire through. Long fibres are just as difficult to carve or trim as nylon fibre can be. On the other hand, the short length of natural cellulose fibre yields more than acceptable green strength as a paper clay. It is also easier to model and form paper clays with shorter fibres. In sum, we ceramicists may use the cellulose fibres that the handmade paper-makers tend to avoid.

Papers and recycled papers good for clay

Composition and structure

Almost any plant or tree could theoretically become a paper if the fibre bundles can be broken down small enough. Paper-makers have probably tried them

all. No matter how long pulp is beaten, after a certain point the fibre strands, tapered at each end, cannot be further broken into pieces without using highly specialised machinery and more toxic chemicals in the water.

The resilient cellulose tubes can take all manner of compression, stretching, abrasion and stress. In fact, it's difficult to destroy cellulose structures unless they are burned. Cellulose fibres, observed under the scanning electron microscope, have abrasive hairy surfaces. In paper, cellulose tubes are seen scrambled, entangled, compressed, and finally dried out as a sheet. In theory then, papers could be recycled forever but for the fact that the ink compounds stain the white surface. The search for a safe, nontoxic

Ceramic book from *Books That Can't be Opened!* by Rosette Gault (USA).

method of ink separation is a topic of much research in recycled paper technology. Most papers with ink do not concern the ceramicist because the inks burn off during the firing.

Paper selection criteria – 6 questions

To evaluate a paper which I am considering using to make into a pulp ceramic clay, I ask myself the following questions:

Do I have the time and the desire to recycle?

You need at least 20 minutes of extra time for the recycling process once you have the paper and a mixing system worked out. Allow a lot more time than that if you are a beginner or you use a more difficult paper. You will need a decent quality drill,[3] a proper mixing blade tool[4] and clean extra buckets in the studio.

Before investing in the tools and time needed to recycle, test a small batch as follows: use purchased toilet tissue rolls but remove the cardboard tube. (This type of Western-style toilet tissue may not be available in all parts of the world, however.) You might need about one to four rolls to start with. Most rolls of toilet paper should dissolve to instant pulp by hand agitation in a bucket of warm water. Western-style paper towels are not advisable because they have very long fibres which are difficult to break up into pulp. One good thing about toilet rolls is that it's easy to keep track of how many rolls you used for a batch and adjust your recipes accordingly.

How much of the paper do I need?

A carton or two of out of date brochures from the neighbourhood print shop can be added to many gallons, litres, pounds or kilo batches of clay. If the source of shredded paper is the office upstairs, a plastic garbage (bin) bag will last quite a while. If the paper supply changes, so will your pulp. If the source is your local newspaper, a few days' worth minus the coated colour inserts will probably suffice to start. Or, if you use household papers, recycled egg cartons or scraps from the drawing table will do. However, a consistent source of paper will help you to establish more accurate recipes for yourself over time.

Is this paper non-glossy or coated?

Coated papers and glossy papers will take ages to dissolve and break down, so I avoid them. Beware especially of the coated newsprint advertisement inserts if they are mixed in with plain black and white newsprint. But glossy, clay coated papers in the really fine magazines can be used dipped in clay slip to make 'paper kilns' (an example of one is shown on p.95, and discussed on p.102)[5].

How easy is the paper to tear?

The easier paper is to tear, the faster it will be to dissolve in water to make pulp.

Is there printing or colour on the paper?

About 99% of all inks and coloured papers will burn away in the kiln. If you wish, test fire a small sample of white clay body as a paper clay to temperature to know for sure. In the rare cases where the ink has made a difference, the clay usually fires slightly more tan in colour than normal.

What condition is your paper in?

Watch out for staples, paper clips, adhesive tape, and metals in shredded office papers. What a disappointment after the final firing to see an unplanned black patch appear on an otherwise pure white paper clay surface, or worse, to nick your skin on a piece of metal. Cellophane windows on envelopes don't dissolve, while cardboard is full of hard glues that maintain their integrity even under studio conditions. However, thin carbon tissues mixed in with cheap, tractor-feed green stripe computer paper seem to dissolve well with plenty of blending. A batch of highly shredded colour coated magazine stock may eventually break down with persistent mixing and straining in hot water. If you have limited tools, this process can be tedious.

Even though different pulps may be used in the same clay, sort the papers first. Make pulp in batches by paper type, e.g. newsprints separate from old brochures, or long or short fibre papers separate from one another.

Sources of papers to 'recycle'

Like many types of clay, different varieties of paper are suitable pulp for different ceramic bodies. Each paper will have a slightly different type of cellulose, and many papers also have small proportions of clay in their composition that could raise the firing temperature.

As described in the table (see p.118) there are many potential sources of paper that could be recycled in your clay. Store-bought materials such as sheets of pure cellulose, blotter paper, or bags of papier maché pulp are in my opinion a waste of money, though they will perform well. Fluffy cellulose for building insulation is convenient but be aware that toxic fumes from fire retardants will continue coming off for hours in the firing. The fire retardant (boric acid) keeps the cellulose from burning until nearly 800°–900°C (1472°–1652°F) far beyond the normal flash point of paper (around 250°C/482°F).

Advance preparation: the mixing tools

To disperse and separate the individual fibres of the pulp in the water, attach a long-shaft propeller mixing blade to a heavy-duty 1 cm (⅜ in.) size or larger electric drill. The best mixing blade may come from your local cement supplier, and look something like the one shown in the photograph on p.32. This tool is great for other uses around the workshop, such as mixing up glazes and slips. Note: paint mixers don't have enough surface area on their blades to efficiently break down pulp.

Some varieties of pulp water may be irritating to the skin during pulp making, especially if you use hot water, so have rubber gloves handy. Also, eye goggles are a good precaution. For safety, avoid standing on a wet floor if you are holding the power-mixing tool when it is plugged in.

Pulp preparation

Converting papers to pulp

Once the papers are sorted, gather various empty clean buckets around you and be near a water source and drain. Fill a bucket no more than ¾ full with warm or hot water. When the rotary drill blades start to break the paper into pulp, the level will probably rise up the sides, depending on the power of the drill. If you have filled the bucket too full of water it could overflow.

If you use toilet rolls you don't need warm water, but for almost all other pulp making use as hot a water as you can stand. Use gloves if necessary. If anything, use more water than you think you will need as the more watery and soupy the pulp mix is, the faster the pulp breaks down. The less water and more paper you use, the longer it will

ABOVE; LEFT Tear up newspaper into small bits and soak in hot water. Do not mix in different types of paper together at this stage. (Other types of paper can also be used – see Appendix.) CENTRE Turn toilet paper into pulp.

First, remove the cardboard tube from inside the roll. Dip the toilet paper completely into water to soak it through. RIGHT Tear off wet chunks from the toilet paper and add them to the bucket.

take to get good quality pulp.

If using shredded paper, just fill the barrel about ⅓ full of shreds, and then fill with water until it is about ⅔–¾ from the top. If using newsprint, tear 2.5–5 cm (1–2 in.) strips. The ratio is then about ⅓ floating paper in a ¾ full bucket of water.

For old brochures or thicker card papers, tear them into squares about 2.5–5 cm (1–2 in.) and let them drop into the water. Beware – these high quality compressed papers sometimes expand like a sponge in the water and really fluff up. Only fill the bucket about ⅕ full with paper, and ¾ full of water to start, and adjust ratios later.

For artist's papers, tear into 2.5–5 cm (1–2 in.) pieces and depending on the paper quality (i.e. cellulose content), fill about ¼–⅓ of a bucket which should already be approximately ¾ full of water.

For toilet paper, use only one roll at first to a ¾ full water bucket of the 20 litre size (4–5 gallon). Each brand of toilet tissue roll seems to yield a different amount of pulp.

Several years ago, computer paper was a short fibre paper. The cheapest papers

dissolved the easiest and fastest. Laser copies were still relatively rare. Nowadays computer laser printer papers are what they call 'long fibre' and these, even as a shredded paper, take much longer to dissolve. Furthermore, the high-tech laser printers and some of the high end copy machines now have such intense concentrations of ink on the surface (up to 600 or more dpi). When these papers start to dissolve in water, whole letters float off the surface like alphabet soup and bubbly ink scum appears on the water surface. None of this will hurt the pulp, or affect the clay. It used to be that computer papers broke down in about five minutes of motorised mixing. Now, the time to pulp some laser printed papers may be extended to 30 minutes or more.

To prepare pulp

Mix the paper and water until it looks like runny soup and you can't read any of the printed letters in the text any more. The water and ink may stain the pulp,

but the stain is usually temporary. When pulp breakdown is complete, the floating pulp should look a little like fluffy clouds in the sky, and the pulp should feel soft, like wet lint in your hand. At a certain point, no matter how long you continue to mix, the pulp won't dissolve any further. In some cases, there may be little soft clouds and no evidence of hard paper bits and pieces, but undissolved bits may show up later, perhaps when a wire is run through the clay. This partially dissolved

BELOW Pulp when it is too wet (left), just about right (centre), and too dry (right).

ABOVE Pulp mixing – using a rotary drill and mixing blade to achieve a fluffy pulp condition.

pulp will burn away in the kiln, but may leave pock marks on your clay. The best paper clays have no visible paper pieces.

If it seems as if the pulp is taking forever to dissolve, you may have mixed two different fibre lengths or types of paper together in the same bucket. If so, you may not want to wait for the longer fibre to break down. Start over with just one type of paper. If you did use the same type of paper to start then you may have skimped on the water. The

remedy is to double or triple the amount of water to pulp ratio. Pulp water can be thin and runny like a gruel. Perhaps if you used cold water, warm or hot water may speed up the process.

Another remedy for paper that's taking too long to pulp is to change the water. Strain and rub the pulp by hand in the sieve. Put the sieved, pebbly pulp back into fresh warm or hot water. Mix the pulp a second time and you will notice a definite improvement in the breakdown. Repeat as necessary for stubborn fibres.

Don't leave pulp soaking in water for more than a few days, depending on the weather. Moulds and a smell may develop.

Once you have the pulp dissolved to your satisfaction, there are several choices. I add a couple of tablespoons of household bleach or disinfectant to large barrels if I think I'm going to need more than a week or two of time. The addition of bleach or disinfectant will only slow the growth of moulds and fungi, it will not prevent them. Moulds and fungi grow more quickly in heat, and also more quickly with recycled fibres than with virgin fibres.

If you are a beginner, sieve your pulp with a household mesh sieve or screen

When the pulp appears wet and fluffy, a kitchen sieve serves as a strainer to extract the pulp. Scoop the pulp out, letting the water drain off.

but don't squeeze out too much water. Handfuls of wet pulp will do fine for use in thick paste slips as the photograph shows (see p. 34). For use in casting slips or slips that are runny, more water may be squeezed out. If you squeeze out so much water that you have pebbly nuggets of pulp, this form of pulp is good for storage in airtight plastic bags (two weeks to one month average at room temperature). Or, you can freeze the pulp indefinitely for future use. When it's time to use again, you should thaw and re-soak the pulp before use.

Pulps made from different papers can be blended together after complete breakdown, but not before. Each paper type seems to break down at its own rate in the pulp/water making stage.

Making p'slip into paper clay and vice versa

Measuring and mixing p'slip

Fill a bucket about $2/3$ to $3/4$ full of thick clay slip made from the base clay formula churned to a smooth and creamy consistency, or substitute a ready-made casting slip. Add wet pulp by handfuls, stirring it in as you go until the slip resembles a thick oatmeal. By eye, or with a measuring stick, you can judge the approximate proportion of pulp to slip that you have used. From 10–40% by volume is common, but as little as 2% and as much as nearly double the volume of the clay slip has been used. You'll need about 25–32% by volume in most clays to get better wet over dry ability. More specific guidelines and custom recipes are explained in the next chapter and on p. 134.

Dissolve the pulp in the slip as uniformly as possible. The purpose of starting with fluid clay slip is to coat and surround each strand of cellulose evenly. The oatmeal textured paper clay slip is then poured out on plaster slabs and left to dry out to the desired soft consistency for wedging. If the oatmeal texture of the paper clay slip is too runny, let the excess water evaporate over time or sponge it off the top as it rises to the surface in the bucket.

Another way to make paper clay is to know ahead of time how much water will be required for the volume of dry clay on hand. Make pulp in this amount of water but do not strain the pulp. Rather, dissolve dry mix clay directly in the pulp water.

In Soldner-style or cement/dough mix machinery, people report adding wet pulp with the measured water to the dry ingredients as they mix. If you wish to try this, consider pre-mixing a portion of the clay slip with the pulp beforehand to pre-coat the fibres. Studio-made pulp fibres are likely to clog up most vacuum de-airing pug mills so mix in pug mills at your own risk. If you do use machinery, mix for as long a time as possible without the paper

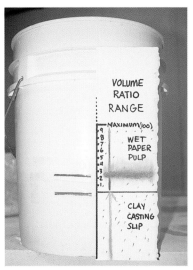

ABOVE Recycled pulp differs, so fine-tune the ratio of clay to pulp for your base clay and purpose.

clay drying out too much. Aim for uniform saturation of the cellulose fibres with water and clay. In a machine, do not mix paper clay too stiff, or wedge it up too dry. Most recipes respond best as a softer mix.

BELOW; LEFT 1. For a sculpture blend, fill a similar bucket with 8 units (or 8 in. in volume) of creamy smooth casting slip (or smooth potter's slurry). CENTRE 2. Start to add the pulp – as shown floating on the surface. The level will start to rise. The more pulp added the better for repair work, and

the lighter the work will be after firing.
RIGHT 3. Finish adding pulp (note how much the level has risen). Next, stir in by hand or tool so that all the fibres soak and separate, and the mix resembles oatmeal. Any excess water is sponged off the next day from the top of the bucket.

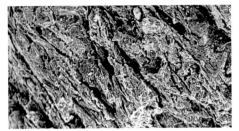

ABOVE Pour fresh p'slip onto a plaster surface and let it stiffen before wedging.

RIGHT; TOP SEM 35% (volume) pulp/bone dry.
CENTRE Close-up of above.
BOTTOM SEM of paper clay fired to 700°C (30% pulp by volume) – Note fibre voids.
SEM photographs courtesy of David Kingery, University of Arizona.

Pulp proportion guidelines

Once you have a sense of your intentions, base clay and type of pulp, you can estimate an appropriate starting proportion and adjust from there. See also the Appendix for details on adjusting the base clay recipe.

Notes

1 Actually the lignin compounds (ligno-sulphates) have a limited affinity for water compared to cellulose. Put simply: lignin chemically traps a certain amount of water. This trapped water tends not to evaporate easily. Excess water remaining in the cellulose proper has a different chemistry and flows easily through the plant tissue.
2 Lignins, when extracted from pulp, have a wide variety of uses for soil binders, fillers, resin extenders and hardeners as well as linoleum adhesives. Lignins may be processed with sodium, magnesium, calcium and ammonia and other metal salts. Orzan previously mentioned as a non-shrink clay body binder is in fact a lignin.
3 The adjustable speed drill should be a heavy-duty one that can take between five to ten minutes of continuous operation.
4 The tool should have lots of blade surface area. Cheaper paint mixer tools don't chop the fibre well. See Appendix for tool suggestions.
5 Paper kilns are described in more detail in various magazines.

Chapter Three

Types of Paper Clay

Most base clay recipes convert easily to paper clay. Distinction between the well-known clay groups may help fine tune how much pulp to add. Variables such as availability of material, intended purpose, clay texture, handling capability, equipment in the studio, firing temperature, kilns, weather, etc. will affect the recipe. Judge the volume of pulp proportion by eye or by a ruler in the bucket.

Versions of well-known clays

Low-fire clay group (900°–1150°C/ 1652°–2102°F)

Earthenware, terracotta, raku and low-fire

These paper clays are usually very open and lightweight and good for small or large projects. Almost all earthenware paper clays need to be bisqued to at least 1000°C (1832°F), but even earthenware paper clay can be raku fired. Because earthenware clay can be so open, use glaze to 'seal' the pores if necessary. High pulp earthenware paper clay, even if vitrified, may seep water, so test fire a few cones higher than normal.

Most white earthenware talc bodies as paper clay, even though rated to cone 04–05, can be fired up to cone 6 before they melt or warp, so before attempting a larger project always test fire. Some high pulp paper clay earthenwares are surprisingly hard and vitreous and resemble porcelains at about 1168°–1250°C/

2166°–2282°F). Again the result depends on the amount and type of pulp you have used. Also, ball/talc bodies can have higher proportions of pulp than most other clay types.

If you want to try detailed dry carving or trim work, try a 'sinter set' fire first (this is explained further in the section on carving). An earthenware paper clay for sculpture that is rock hard and can survive freezing and snow outdoors was developed at the University of Delaware under the supervision of Victor Spinski (see Appendix for recipe, p.136).

Raku, pit fire, saggar clays

Almost all forms of paper clay are suitable for raku, pit or saggar fires. Add medium to high levels of pulp to otherwise shatter-prone porcelain, earthenware, talc and casting slip-based paper clays for raku. Pre-bisque when possible. Preheat glazed greenware for single firing. Some paper clay bodies can even withstand wet firing.

High-fire group (1150°C/2102°F plus)

Stoneware as paper clay

Most stoneware will perform as usual. Bisque medium to high pulp paper clay to at least 1000°C (1832°F) for easier handling. Consider the notes below for porcelains and chamotte clays. Higher amounts of pulp improve workability of wet over dry. Beige fired tints from some of the inked pulps will blend with the colour of most stoneware. The Marsh Report[1] (see also p.121) suggests that an all-purpose stoneware that has minimum deformation at high temperatures should have 20% volume pulp and 20% PG grog (a fine grain chamotte).

Porcelains as paper clay

Most delicate forms with porcelain paper clay survive the bisque temperatures. However, this initial success can give a false sense of confidence. The stress of high temperature firing these porcelain clays so close to their melting points is extreme. Construct forms with adequate reinforcement and support in the kiln. Thin walls of some porcelains may 'move' or 'warp' as early as 1200°–1250°C/2192°–2282°F (around cone 6). Well-engineered forms will survive however. There is more information about structural reinforcements on pp.51–2.

Some wood pulps in porcelain can cause a trace of colour shift in the 'white' and/or celadon[2]. Porcelains need a higher bisque, to at least 1000°C (1832°F). At low bisque (900°–1000°C/1652°–1832°F), carve and precision trim soft porcelain figures with metal tools.

Paper clay porcelain will shrink in firing as is normal for porcelains (this can be up to 20%). To reduce the chance of deformation in porcelains at high temperatures, the Marsh Report recommends for a 20% pulp paper clay porcelain to alter the base recipe as follows: increase the kaolin 5% and reduce both the spar 3% and the flint 2% for the minimum deformation. Most porcelain paper clay I have worked with is dense and vitreous above 1250°C. Glaze as usual. At around 1250°–1275°C (2282°–2327°F), the ash-filled network of fibre voids within the porcelain starts to liquefy to a glaze.[3] The voids fill in and collapse gradually in the heat. More

research and electron micrographs on this would be helpful.

Speciality clay groups – saggars, bricks

Saggar clays have to withstand multiple 'saggar' firings. Saggars are stacking cases used to protect pots inside the kiln from the direct flame during firing. Saggar clays, like bricks, already have half the volume as an additive. Replace as much percentage as desired with pulp, but observe the half and half volume limit. Bricks of paper clay are, in my opinion, a form of highly refined adobe. An unusual example of paper clay 'bricks' being used can be seen in Chapter 9, p.108.

Paper clay custom recipes

The best paper clay base for your work will most likely come from one of the traditional groups mentioned above. Studio-made paper clay formulation allows further control of common preferences such as texture, pulp ratio and purpose of the clay batch.

1. The texture and composition of the parent clay

In the hand, parent clays feel either smooth or gritty. This basic distinction will not change in the paper clay version. Texture can affect a paper clay recipe as follows.

Fine-grained clays *without* chamotte, grog, sand, etc.

Ultra fine-grained clays are less abrasive to the hands when modelling or throwing. The expanded capacity for alteration and green strength will be dramatic compared to a non-paper clay. Carve crisp, sharp detail if desired.

Make fine grain p'slip easily from a base of ready-mixed casting slip. Less water in

LEFT *Papier-Porcelaine, wall work* by Jean-Paul Béranger (France), 1987.

the only choice to reduce cracking, help green strength, and 'open up' a clay. Cellulose can do many of these same jobs. In paper clays, additives of 'non-plastic' large grain non-clay fillers to clay recipes are acceptable in moderate amounts. These can provide useful colour or texture to your fired clay.

If the parent clay contains near the maximum possible amounts of chamotte or filler, reduce the amount of pulp or chamotte proportionately so that the over-all ratio of clay to 'filler' is not extreme. It is impossible to give an exact recipe here due to the wide variety of clays sculptors might use. Try about 10–50% by volume of filler, pulp or both in combination. In most paper clays, for good wet over dry, about 25–35% by volume of pulp is suggested.

2. The type and combination of pulp

The grade of cellulose fibre, the lignin content and the fibre length will all affect the network of air voids left after the pulp burns out (we can call it the fired 'loft'). Consistent 'loft' from batch to batch may concern the paper clay maker who has to change pulp source in the middle of a large project. Keep in mind that each pulp or combination of pulps will have a slightly different 'loft' effect on the interior of the clay. For example 20% by volume of pulp made from paper A might be equivalent to 30% of pulp from paper B. A table is supplied in the Appendix. Most of the time this won't be critical to you unless you are planning multiple consistent batches such as in large-scale works or production.

It is easy to mix and match different loft percentages of not only the same clay, but also of similar clays in a certain maturing temperature range. For

the p'slip usually means less waiting time for this type of p'slip to dry on plaster. A more dense packing of casting slip clay particles per centimetre around the fibres of paper clay can cause the fired strength to extend further in high pulp recipes than expected.[4] Nevertheless, as in the notes for porcelains, take special care to engineer the construction of the form to withstand the stress of the fire, especially above 1100°C (2012°F).

Chamotte, grog or sand sawdust, vermiculite, in your paper clay

To make gritty textured paper clays, add roughage in the form of various non-plastic 'fillers' to the recipe. In the past, chamotte and sand were routinely added in rather high amounts to many clays. Chamotte and grog used to be considered

38

example, as paper clays, white earthenware talc bodies can be joined with terracotta red earthenware. Stoneware and most porcelains can be joined also.

The affinity between lignins and specific clays is a topic for future research. Both virgin and inked (i.e. recycled) wood pulps with high lignin may improve certain properties of ceramic paper clays such as fired strength.

3. The purpose of the clay batch

Paper clay conversion lessens some distinctions between sculpture, wheel and casting clay bodies. The boundaries extend as follows.

Sculpture

Paper clay bodies for sculpture, like conventional clays, can have a full variety of particle sizes and fillers, or 'non-plastic' material in the recipe.

Even fine-grained paper clay conversions will suit large sculptures provided the pulp content, engineering and firing are within guidelines. In other words, grog for strength is an option, not a requirement, especially for low firing (below cone 6).

At the extreme end of the sculpture spectrum would be the high loft, ultra 'open' paper clay recipe at half volume of pulp. However, these recipes may be crumbly and less durable. In the majority of cases, high-pulp clays will mature or harden at a higher temperature than normal. The high-pulp recipes will be increasingly less plastic to work with as the proportion of pulp increases. However, for large volume lightweight inner structures, a high-pulp recipe is superb.

The far low end of the spectrum is the ratio of 1–2% volume of pulp to clay.

There will be some increase in green strength, but most of the other features such as wet over dry capability will not be reliable. Until more pulp is in the recipe, this form of paper clay is very 'clay'-like. (The higher the concentration of pulp, the less cracking during drying will occur.)

The chart on p.120 suggests good blends for starting points for different purposes. For sculpture innards, consider high levels of pulp blend. For sculpture exterior layers, consider a medium pulp 'shell' layer. Use medium to high pulp for large and small-scale figures. For tiles, a low to medium level, and for wall hangings, a high-pulp content can be tolerated. For those who plan outdoor sculptures that must survive freezing and snow, review the information under the earthenware section earlier in this chapter.

Covered Jar by Jerry Bennett (USA),
salt-fired porcelain.

Paper clay bodies will survive such conditions only when the base recipe can. More
testing in this area would be helpful.

Paper clay and the potter's wheel

For the wheel-throwing process, use
homogenous, wedged paper clay.
Throwing bodies are usually best with
low to medium levels of pulp. Pugged up
commercial grades of either 'sculptor's' or
'thrower's' paper clay may throw surprisingly well. Although paper clay on the
wheel immediately generates some fibrous
slurry, experienced throwers are able to
adapt to this. Paper clay on the wheel
does not 'stretch' the same as conventional clay either, but pulled handles are fine
in low-pulp varieties. Paper clay has its
own feel, both similar and dissimilar to

potter's clay. Change some work habits if
necessary. Some throwers use paper clay
for teapots and other large complex
assemblies. Repair of any 's' cracks and
assembly of bone dry parts is possible. The
more you reduce the pulp ratio to get a
more 'clay-like' paper clay, the more you
sacrifice the wet on dry capacity. Personal
taste will be the key.

There are two types of commercially
prepared paper clay for throwing: 1) The
basic all-purpose 'sculptor's' version is
similar to the paper clay described in this
book. As a throwing body, this paper clay
has green strength and will be excellent
for larger or tall works. The 'sculptural'
forms of paper clay need to be trimmed
with sharp tools. Commercially prepared, ready-made pugs in plastic bags
may soon be available in your area.
2) A 'potter's' version of commercially-
made paper clay that is easy to trim is
available in some areas.

Paper clays for casting

Casting clay-based recipes should meet
the following criteria: 1) be smooth
pouring; 2) will respond to dispersal
easily; 3) will set up as quickly as possible in a plaster mould; 4) will release
easily from a plaster mould; 5) will be as
strong as possible as a greenware; 6) can
be fettled or sponged easily; 7) will have
the right fired colour.

These criteria somewhat limit the
choice of ceramic clays that can be used
as a base. Dispersal electrolyte chemicals, added to the water, work better
with the non-iron bearing materials and
flat particle sized mixtures normally
used. If the potential base slip contains
bentonite, certain fire clays or kaolin or
red iron oxides, it may not be easy to get
the slip to pour in a smooth ribbon (see
Chapter 2 and the Appendix for more
information).

When cellulose is added to casting bodies, it affects the chemistry for casting. In most cases cellulose improves the strength of the casting and shortens the waiting time for release and peel off. In addition, work may be repaired, altered and assembled wet over dry. For more information see the section on moulds in Chapter 7.

Studio-made p'slip must be of the right consistency (like oatmeal) to cast up well. If the p'slip is too thick to start with, the casting may lack some areas of detail. The plaster also should be of the right moisture content to get smooth detail on the surface of the casting. The studio-made variety of p'slip can be smeared into open slipcast style moulds. The castings will be quite strong and may release sooner than normal, so trim with fettle or scissors and remove from the mould at leather or leatherhard stage. When a studio-made casting is bone dry, fettling is more difficult and

Commercially manufactured selection of 'Sculpture' and 'Potters' P'Clays'™ and 'Basic' and 'Casting' P'Slips'™ are made to order.

requires a sharp tool. All the detail will be there however, provided the p'slip was in a fluid condition when poured.

Conventional slipcasting and pouring with studio-made 'oatmeal' paper clay will be cumbersome at best. Commercial casting recipes show great promise for easy fettling and smooth pouring.[6] Moulds are more fully discussed from p.85 onwards.

Notes

1 Ginny Marsh at the University of Louisville, Kentucky, conducted research to determine pulp limits for reduction of high-fire porcelain and stoneware deformation. The Appendix includes a table of distinctions between types of cellulose and amounts needed in a recipe.

2 *High Fire Porcelain and Stoneware Paper Clay*, Report by Ginny Marsh, University of Louisville, Kentucky, 1995 (published in first edition of *Paper Clay*). For example, some recipes for blue celadon glaze shifted blue-green in paper clay porcelain and the clay bodies had a more yellow tint. Fired translucency will be retained where clay is thin. If adjustment is necessary, check that your parent clay recipe has room for more additive. A heat threshold for porcelains was noticed at around 1220°C (2228°F). Beyond this, temperature slumping was possible. (See p.121.)

3 Ash is a natural flux or melting agent for silica at these temperatures. I expect that on the micrograph level we would see a tiny shell of glaze form around each tube void of cellulose within a matrix of growing mullite crystals.

4 If you add more than 5% pulp by weight, fired strength tends to weaken according to strength testing conducted by Leena Juvonens for the University of Industrial Arts, Helsinki, Finland, 1995.

5 See Appendix for details about licensing, trademark and distribution worldwide. Patents on the commercial manufacture process are pending.

6 For information about commercially prepared 'Casting' P'Slip™ contact New Century Arts, which can be found in the list of suppliers on p.141.

42

Chapter Four

What Paper Clays Can Do

In the following chapters we shift from the technical view of paper clay to the hands-on perspective. Now that paper clay and p'slip are ready in the studio – what next? This chapter describes features common to all paper clays. Chapter 5 revisits the well-established legacy of handbuilding and wheel work, Chapters 6 and 7 discuss paper clay as it can be used in sculpture and Chapter 8 the surfaces and firing specifications of paper clays.

Paper clay to wedge

To get a supply of wedged homogenous paper clay, pour a thick layer of p'slip on a large plaster batt. Wedge when the thick paste is just turning to a soft putty consistency. The amount of water in the p'slip and plaster slab affects the evaporation rate. To 'speed wedge', scrape the excess p'slip off the top of the plaster slab several minutes or so after you have poured it. With a flexible rubber rib, immediately lift or scrape up the ultra soft layer of paper clay beneath.

LEFT *Angel* in progress by Dave Porter, Archie Bray Foundation, (Montana, USA), 1996.

RIGHT After pouring p'slip over plaster, leave it to dry out a little. If you do not want to wedge your clay you can scrape it off the plaster bat using a rubber rib or kidney (which will not scratch the plaster) and use the 'putty-like' substance immediately to model with.

For best results, wedge when the clay is as moist as possible. High-pulp clay may feel a little more like 'putty' than you are used to and, when paper clay has a high-pulp content or is too dry, it may seem a little shorter than normal. Experience and personal taste are the key. If your clay gets too dry to wedge or handle easily, save it (dried out) for miscellaneous use as stiff supports or as appendages in future sculptures.

Work surfaces

A variety of work surfaces are suitable for paper clays. Plaster slabs for drying p'slip should be clean, smooth and water absorbent. The surface of the plaster should not be sealed or coated. If there is

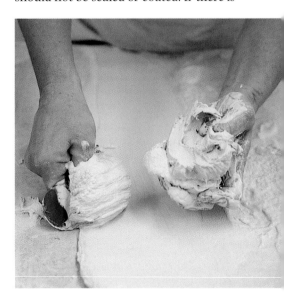

too little moisture in the plaster, the p'slip dries too quickly and might stick. To remedy this, wipe a damp sponge over the ultra dry slab. Or pour a super thick layer of p'slip on super-dry slabs for the first use. If the plaster is too wet or uncured, p'slip will not dry out. In the Appendix you will find more information about plaster.

Slabs of soft paper clay rolled out over non-absorbent linoleum or formica surfaces will dry slowly. Details on paper clay slabs are discussed in the next chapter. Surfaces such as wood, linen or canvas-covered tabletops and bisque will tend to dry the paper clay. Press-mould paper clay (not p'slip) into bisque ware. P'slip over absorbent surfaces, especially over bisque, will be very difficult to release, unless you place a layer of tissue in between. To dry out large batches of p'slip, prop a plaster slab from below so that air can circulate. P'slip dries more quickly on plaster dry-wall or cement floors surfaces than on linoleum.

Joins and adhesion of paper clays

With conventional clay you normally join and assemble two pieces of leather-hard and/or soft clay by scratching marks on the surfaces to be joined and using a layer of slip as adhesive. It is imperative with conventional clay to make joins before the clay dries out completely. *With paper clay you can join soft or leatherhard or even bone dry clay to itself or in some cases to bisque.* The key is simple. Replenish some of the moisture in the bone dry or bisque each time you make an alteration with fresh p'slip and/or paper clay combinations. A wet or watery environment at the contact point is necessary for cellulose fibre and clay (fired or bisque) to knit together and bond.

To prepare the bone dry for adhesion, either dip the bone dry work area directly in the water bucket for a few seconds or, if dipping is impractical, brush generous spongefuls of plain water over the surface. Water spray will work also. Apply layers of p'slip over the wet surface before you adhere soft paper clay additions. Blend soft paper clay into the wet surface. For weight-bearing joints, scratch the wet surfaces to be joined with a serrated rib or needle for the best possible join (see pp. 51–2).

How is this wet over dry joining possible? A capillary network of interwoven cellulose tubes within both paper clay and p'slips allows for water to circulate and to drain. Water in the p'slip 'thick oatmeal' will be absorbed and sucked down into the 'thirsty' surface of the bone dry part. Wet ends of each fibre (cellulose) follow the current and start to poke down dry pores too. The fibre ends stiffen in the process of evaporation and dispersion of water. The resulting 'grip' between dry and wet resembles Velcro.

In addition, adhesive lignins in most pulps have a high chemical affinity for clay mineral colloidal particles.

RIGHT *Columns* by Grace Nickel (Canada), height: 214 cm (7 ft).
Paper clay is a revolutionary concept and certainly has allowed for changes in my work… I pounded a hammer on dry sheets of paper clay until they had a beautiful cracked and aged appearance. All this abuse and the sheet remained intact in the dry stage! The next step was to moisten them around the edges and adhere them to the leatherhard column… after applying terra sigillata and firing, they had a wonderful, prehistoric, bony look, just what I wanted!… amazing indeed!

45

Bird by Kathy Ross (USA), 1996, 51 × 31 × 31 cm (20 × 12 × 12 in.).

Carving and trimming

You can carve, chisel or saw paper clays in all states and conditions, both before and in some cases after low-temperature sinter or bisque fires (see p.135 and p.48). The paper fibres will normally be too small to be visible in the fired surface. Carving on paper clay is versatile as repair, addition and alteration is nearly always possible.

Bone dry strength will enable you to carve on delicate forms.

The pulp concentration, moisture content and parent clay itself all affect the amount of pressure needed on your carving tool. The drier the paper clay, the more you will notice paper fibre on your tool when you carve. Sponge the leather or bone dry clay with water periodically to soften the work area as you dig. Expect the trim to be a fine but fibrous powder. To carve paper clays with a lot of grit, perlite, sand and/or chamotte at bone dry or leather, sponge water onto the surface to soften it.

Some sculptors carve hollow areas out of solid clay to lighten and strengthen the structure. This practical system, mandatory for conventional clay, is only one of many options with high green strength paper clays. The walls of paper clay structures normally do not have to be an even thickness and, when dry, will support the extra weight of wet layers. Fast drying and the chance to rebuild over the dry can be used in combination with the more traditional carving techniques when working with paper clays. The more pulp and/or other additives in the body, the more difficult the clay might be to carve, but even this can be compensated for by a sinter set or bisque fire.

Sinter set carving

Low-temperature earthenware and terracotta paper clays can be sinter set fired to about 540°C (1004°F), which is a temperature too low for most cones to detect but measurable with pyrometers and/or kiln computers. The sinter temperature is just before the quartz inversion. Cellulose fibres should have vaporised at about 253°C (451°F). Sinter carve marks on the fine-grained clays and particularly the earthenware yields a fine non-fibrous clay powder. There is no drag on your metal carving tool from the paper fibre.

Sinter set fire is also an excellent means of setting certain crumbly glazes and engobes. Apply colour brushwork over the 'sinter set' glaze beneath. Refire to maturing temperature afterwards.

Bisque carving

You can continue to carve ultra crisp lines, detail and trim at bisque with certain paper clays. The line-grained high-fire porcelains, china clays and stoneware

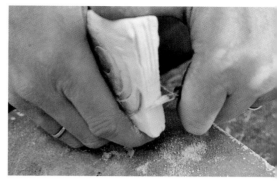

Use a *flat* knife to get ultra crisp edges when carving a sintered porcelain or earthenware (fine-grain smooth paper clay). 'Sintering' is a fire just hot enough (550°C/1000°F) to burn all fibres of paper out – but not too hot to dull the blade.

Use a *curved* knife trim blade to get ultra crisp detail perfection in 'sintered' porcelain curves and contours.

paper clays are usually soft enough at low bisque temperatures (900°–1000°C/ 1652°–1832°F) to carve. Those who make prototypes and production originals will find this trim feature useful. If the parent clay contained a high percentage of chamotte or other grainy additive, carving will leave a rough and gritty surface. Earthenware and terracotta paper clays may be too dense at high bisque to carve. Motorised rotary micro drilling Dremel-style tools may give you favourable results on some bisque-fired paper clays.

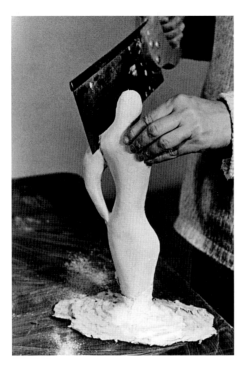

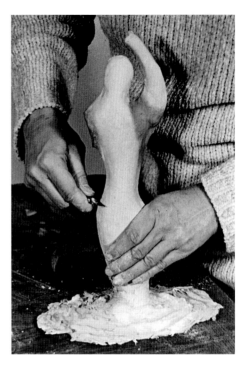

Cut bone dry paper clay arm with a saw, then place arm in new position with water, p'slip and paper clay.

Carve trim on bone dry paper clay with metal blade.

BELOW; LEFT AND RIGHT Score bone dry paper clay with a needle and snap ends apart as you would glass or drywall. *Photographs by Sue Hungerford.*

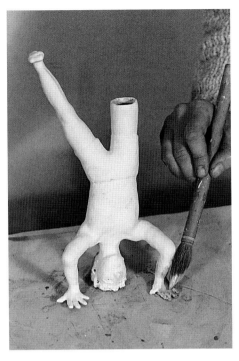

Two slabs being joined together by a wetter paper clay coil in the centre.

Broken bisque finger repair: moistening the area first with water and p'slip.

Repair of broken leg.

BELOW; LEFT AND RIGHT Fresh leather slab is draped over a bone dry paper clay skeleton. Rewet dry structure with a sponge, seal, putty and smooth from below to join. *Photographs by Sue Hungerford.*

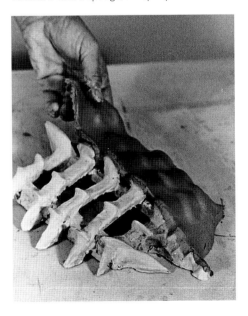

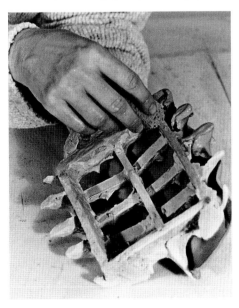

49

Alterations and repairs

Alter, rearrange, disassemble, reassemble, add to, carve down and continue work on paper clay forms for as long as your imagination requires. Suppose a dry paper clay shape needs feet or perhaps a basket handle attached. All of these can be done when the principle of wet over dry assembly is understood (described in detail at the beginning of this chapter under 'Joins'). The higher the pulp percentage in the paper clay, the less chance of cracking. Most cracks in paper clay can be repaired as you go.

Repairs to greenware

In many cases a repair to paper clay greenware will be stronger than the original. Let the piece air-dry if possible. With most shapes, avoid slow drying. With paper clay the stress of the shrinking process during drying in a sense mimics the stress of the firing to come. Each weak area, warp or stress crack that you notice at the bone dry state can and should be reinforced or repaired before the first firing whenever possible. Smaller cracks discovered on dry clay need to be 'wet' again and may be puttied in with p'slip and paper clay.

Paper clay forms are most in danger of warping through the leatherhard to dry stages. Once the form is dry it is not likely to warp further in the kiln unless over-firing occurs. For this reason, assemble bone dry parts wet on dry whenever practical. Most breaks are clean breaks so if the piece is not weight-bearing, simply wet the ends and re-assemble with p'slip and or paper clay.

For broken weight-bearing legs however, build the strongest repair possible. If one side of the break is not already hollow, drill or carve an opening in its centre deep enough proportionally to insert a 'post'. Build a new soft paper clay 'post' (similar in shape to those on many dolls' legs) from the opposite broken end of the leg using wet on dry. Dry out the post and hollow parts separately, force drying them if necessary. Dry parts should nest together in a loose fit. Now, water the dry post and hollow ends a second time. Apply p'slip and paper clay on both ends generously and press and adjust the two parts into place. Finally, smooth off the excess with a damp sponge and let the joint dry once again before adding more weight.

Repairs to bone dry paper clay that involve water, p'slip, and paper clay on each end will normally fare better than those with only p'slip as adhesive. For example, to alter or repair a broken flat hand-built platter, apply water and p'slip to both sides of the break and insert a 1.3 cm ($\frac{1}{2}$ in.) flat soft paper clay coil between the two. Smooth and blend the surface with a damp sponge and/or p'slip and dry out a second time. In this case, the repaired platter will now be about 1.3 cm ($\frac{1}{2}$ in.) wider than before. Platters when fired carry weight and may need reinforcements. Suppose the platter or form is too wide to fit on the kiln shelf. Deliberately break the plate apart, cut or carve it down and reassemble the platter in a smaller version.

Repairs to bisque

A crack in the bisque is a guaranteed loss in conventional clay. However, with paper clay it is usually worth trying to repair most cracks. Broken fingers, noses, ears and tails can usually be rebuilt at bisque, especially with the low-fire clay groups. Bisque repair can be risky – the more practice in application the higher the success rate! Soak the bisque in water

LEFT For high-firing stability reinforce thin areas with a lightweight support material. Fill in a hollow bone dry section with paste of 'Ruff Rock-Gruff Rock' or just p'slip with handfulls of perlite or vermiculite stirred in. RIGHT Work in progress by Rosette Gault. Porcelain eyes and mouth blended with porcelain perlite.

first, apply p'slip and then, if needed, putty in or rebuild as desired with fresh paper clay. As a caution, rebisque after repair to be sure the set is good and the cracks are sealed.

Shira Subotnik deliberately built fresh soft paper clay figures around the edge of a thin walled bisque bowl. Astonishingly, everything made it through not just the second bisque, but to the stoneware firing 1275°C (2327°F).

P'slip may also be used to repair 's' cracks and handle cracks in thrown-ware of either conventional or paper clays. Paper clay bisque responds better to this than non-paper clays. Again, the base clay, pulp percentage, firing procedure and nature of the repair will influence the success or failure of such ventures. The higher the pulp percentage in the parent recipe, the less bisque repair will be necessary.

Reinforcements for inner support
If you make delicate vulnerable forms of high-fire porcelain or stoneware, consider how the form will be supported during the firing. Pulp may give green strength and added handling freedom before firing, while after firing, pulp all but disappears. Also, fired strength may be lost in some, but not necessarily all, of the high-pulp formulae.[1] Many times, adjustment to the parent clay recipe is out of the artist's control, so evaluate how much fired weight thin walls will carry before warping or slumping occurs. I do this by eye and by using my prior experience with the paper clay in question.

Engineer support structures and inner scaffolding supports on delicate paper clay forms *after* the 'shell' is bone dry. One way to build interior support is to dip strips or coils of soft paper clay in p'slip and then adhere them to corners and walls as cross-bracing (see picture of bandage idea on p.71). In some cases, insert a pre-cut dry tube, coil or block for additional scaffolding and/or lattice support. Putty in flimsy areas with paper clay or p'slip. For example, suppose you position a heavy load such as a 'head' on top of a slab arch 'torso'. Although it looks fine at green and bisque, during high-fire, the weight of the clay in the head may be too much for a thin slab arch to support. Relieve the burden of the head on the arch with extra support from within. Hide a new dry tube strong enough to hold the head beneath the torso frame. Make inner reinforcements for larger scale structures with thick but lightweight paper clay strips or coils dipped in p'slip and applied like wet bandages. Use a higher pulp concentration paper clay for inner support if desired.

For finish and trim, when a hollow structure is bone dry, brush generous amounts of runny p'slip over all interior areas. Putty in holes with paper clay. Smooth over rough or sharp edges with a damp sponge for the final trim. Seal structural underpinnings such as these from view with a fresh slab cover if necessary.

Untitled by Trudy Golley (Canada).
Paper clay allows me to challenge my usual ways of working and break the rules. As a result I can work in a direct and spontaneous fashion. (It) gives me freedom to actively push ideas within a medium that will now accommodate them.

Swinging Lemur # 2 by Susan Halls (UK), raku. Yes, paper clay changed my life! I slab, press, coil... do everything with it.

Force drying

Most paper clays can withstand multiple episodes of rewatering with a sponge and force drying too. If you want, force dry medium to high-pulp paper clays with fans, heat guns, hairdryers or kilns (do not exceed 80°C/176°F). It may be appropriate to dry large paper clay sculptures periodically as you work. Otherwise, sealed off wet or thick interior areas in large sculptures can take weeks or months to dry. Force or air-set drying is recommended for large scale works.

Slake down, recycling and storage

To reconstitute dry paper clay into p'slip or paper clay, slake down the smaller dry bits and slab scraps in a bucket of water as you would do with trimmings of conventional clay. Pour the excess water off next day, stir and reuse the p'slip at the bottom of the bucket.

Bone dry paper clay slabs, tubes, and scraps are normally odourless. I pack, transport and store shapes of paper clay in boxes or bags without the extra water weight.

The smell of most older made-up paper clay is mild, except highly-inked pulp clays. The rate at which the smell begins, and the mould grows, the intensity of these side effects varies with the clays, pulps, water and temperature in the mix. I notice that keeping air or light out seems to slow the bacterial growth. To retard the decay process, add a small amount of bleach to the p'slip batch. The smell will go away when the clay is allowed to bone dry and the dark mould colour, if it appears, can be wiped away with a sponge. Mould will usually burn away during the firing. Commercially-prepared P'Slip™ and P'Clay™ have a longer shelf life than a studio-made paper clay, i.e. months rather than weeks.

For these reasons deliberate ageing of paper clay is not recommended. Although aged wet paper clay and p'slip may change smell and colour after a while, it can still be formed and fired. Freezing of the wet paper clay is to be avoided. If it occurs, reprocessing before use may help.[1]

Note

1 Commercially made paper clay and p'slip have controlled specifications on the pulp and preservatives used in their recipes, and have a much longer shelf life. The special pulps used and tested for the commercial varieties must meet federal and state regulations for safety and non-toxic certifications as well.

Chapter Five

Basic Forming Methods

A fresh look

To continue our survey of practical aspects of paper clay, let us take a fresh look at the specific basics of handbuilding and vessel-based ceramics from the perspective of paper clay.

Rays of Revelation and Hope by Tasos Patiniotis (Greece), 120 × 91 cm (47¾ × 35¾ in.), made in Banff, Canada at the Canada-Greece Symposium, 1996. *Photograph by Don Lee.*

Coil

Coil-built pots can be simply made in paper clay, usually without as much elaborate scoring and sealing, provided the coil is soft to begin with. Great heights and thin walls are a tempting possibility. As noted in Chapter 3, thin walls are vulnerable to warping and collapse only if they are overfired.[1] Brush thick or thin p'slip in the cracks of coil forms wet or bone dry as you prefer.

Long uniform coils can be rolled out quite easily with most paper clay bodies. Interweaving, knots, lattices, braiding and patterning with coils is possible. If coils crack up as they are rolled out, try a less absorbent work surface or softer clay to extend coiling work time. If the paper clay is too short to coil well it could be that the base clay recipe is out of balance.[2]

Both paper clay and conventional clay can often be used side by side. Betty Engleholm of Denmark, who makes large garden sculptures and architectural forms, uses a combination of paper clay coils and conventional clay coils. She revives even dried-out conventional clay rims, soaking the rims with wet towels first and applying several inches of paper clay coils and p'slip to serve as a buffer zone. She resumes subsequent coils of conventional clay over the top of the leatherhard paper clay.

Individually made dry coils, rings, knots, interweaving and braiding of any

Coil constructed garden figures by Betty Engleholm (Denmark).

and all description support considerably more weight than usual. Stack and balance bone dry paper clay coils or flattened strips one on top of the other. Tack the 'bones' into temporary position with p'slip during the design phase of construction. To seal, smear the whole structure with generous layers of p'slip and/or paper clay later on in the process. Another unorthodox method is to make oval or circle shapes out of coils but allow these coils to dry out before assembling them. A variety of exotic structures can be built up in successive wet to dry stages in this way.

Pinch

For pinch pots, start with as soft a paper clay as possible. As with normal clay, timing, steady rhythm, and even pressure while pinching are essential. If you let part of the pinch pot set to leather

Slab Towers, freestanding pieces by John Eden.

Slab Towers, detail of a freestanding piece by John Eden. The fired sculptures are substantially lighter but just as strong. The walls of this work are less than 1.3 cm (¹/₂ in.) thick – not bad for pieces that are sometimes 244 cm (8 ft.) tall. Paper clay requires a bit more preparation, but we certainly save in aggravation and shipping costs!

or dry, it will be much easier to build successive pinched structures up as high as the kiln allows. Again, the combination of water, p'slip and paper clay over a dry section makes the best join. To save time, use speed drying if you have a medium to high-pulp paper clay.

Vessels

With paper clay, you can enjoy the extended ability for alterations, work time and surface treatment. For thin walls on vessels or thrown forms, consider the firing atmosphere and maturity of the base clay. The green strength of paper clay is very seductive. However, keep in mind that only the clay itself will remain for structure after firing.

Trimming requires sharp tools and is explained in more detail in Chapter 4.

Handles and detail can be added anytime wet or dry before the final firing, provided the guidelines are understood for working with wet on dry paper clays. Whether a fired paper clay will be watertight depends on variables such as the recipe of the parent clay, the percentage and type of pulp, the glaze surface and the firing condition.[3] Glaze on the interiors and surfaces of vessels fills in microscopic voids and resolves this issue. Most unglazed medium to high-pulp paper clay when fired to maturity will be technically 'vitrified', yet water may nevertheless slowly seep through the foot of

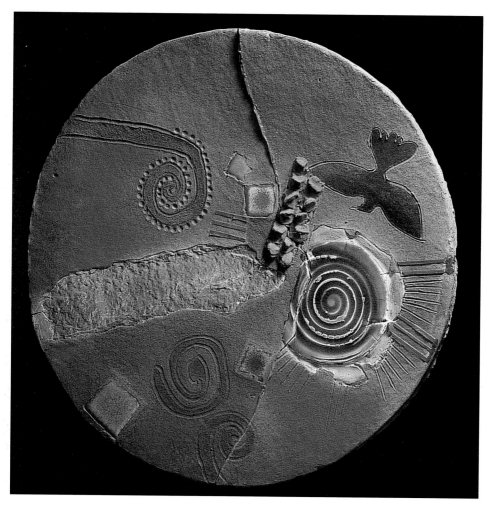

the vessel. More research to find the limits would be helpful.[4] With unglazed paper clays, the more pulp in the recipe, the more water will leak through. Test your recipes to find the best.

The fired strength of paper clay will be comparable to that of base clay in the low-pulp recipes. Fired strength in most paper clay recipes is diminished as the proportion of pulp exceeds 25–30% by volume.[5] Medium-pulp porcelains that I used were just as dense and rocklike strong after firing as the non-pulp base. Results may vary and again, more research will help.

A plate by Brian Gartside (New Zealand), 40 × 60 × 10 cm (15¾ × 23½ × 4 in.). *In the short time of one or two years, sculptural paper clay is becoming a standard way of working for many people and an excellent alternative for others. The thrill of a new way of working is a big attraction to me. In the clay clubs and the societies (in Australia and New Zealand), there has been much passing on of discoveries and methods. Both teachers and students seem to be involved in these experiments. Some artists have been able to seize the techniques and have found that it has extended the scope to their expression by heaps and heaps!*

Wheel work

A millennium of cultural legacy need not necessarily be overturned for the sake of paper clay. Superb conventional clay recipes for the potter's wheel have yielded beautiful results in the hands of expert craftsmen. Nevertheless, paper clay's versatility for wheel work can be habit forming, especially for complex forms such as teapots, handles and multiple assembly pots. Any wheel-made shape or handle you can imagine can be made in paper clay. Repairs and alterations are possible at nearly all stages in the process. Remember though to wedge studio-made paper clay thoroughly for wheel work.

P'clays™, which are relatively soft and not mixed too stiff, respond well on the wheel. Also, most but not all paper clays are more difficult, though not by any means impossible, to trim. Another distinctive feature is an abundance of fibre slurry from throwing. Walls normally hold up well if not overworked. If compression is not uniform on both sides of the wall

Some low-pulp blends are suitable for wheel work, but it is harder to throw than standard clay.

Jon Williams dips greenware bowls in glazes for once-firing to stoneware. The water absorbent bone dry greenware soaks up glaze as if it were bisque without deforming, making it easy to raw fire.

during throwing paper clays, stretch marks may appear in medium to high-pulp batches. Smooth the marks over as soon as you notice them. Expert potters keep moisture to a minimum when throwing and use metal or wood rib tools to help.

Slabs or sheets

In the art studio, there are three principal means of making soft pliant slabs or flat sheets with paper clay and/or p'slip: pouring, rolling or stretching. Flat non-warp slabs and tiles evolve from these. Ram press and extrusion methods with paper clays require a substantial investment in industrial equipment as well as customised recipes.[6]

Soft pliant slabs/sheets

Pour layers of p'slip over a properly made clean plaster surface. Wait until enough water has evaporated for the thickness needed. Scrape and/or smooth

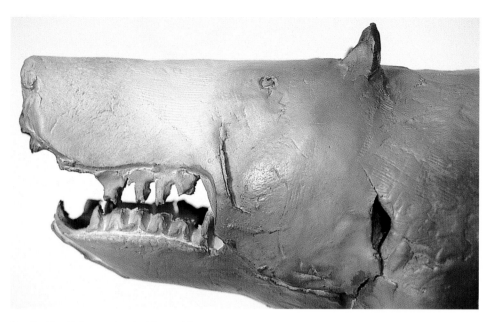

Dog by Sue Halls, constructed from slabs.

off the excess p'slip with a rubber rib. Gently lift or peel the paper clay sheet when the surface is no longer glistening wet, just past the softness best for wedging (see picture on p.63).

To make a soft slab with a roller, lift, rotate, and/or turn over the slab between each compression. To get an even thickness use two wood slats of equal thickness on either edge of the slab to support and limit the roller from pressing the paper clay too thin. If you try to flatten or stretch a soft paper clay slab by 'throwing' the paper clay forcefully down on a table, fibres will inhibit the stretch. The surface of stretched paper clay sheets/slabs may crack into a surface texture. To compensate for stretching, compress and smooth the paper clay surface with a flexible rubber rib as you

Cut fabric or paper shapes and patterns in a soft paper clay slab. Fold the shape while it is pliant – just stiff enough to stand on edge, usually 10 minutes to an hour later.

go along and start with as soft and fresh a paper clay as possible.

To soften paper clay slabs that have dried out, dip or soak them in water. However, beware, as the timing and amount of water reabsorbed in the resoaked slab is critical. Resoftened slabs in my opinion are never quite as pliant as the original.

Shapes and drapes from soft slabs

Cut out shapes in silhouette, either all or part of the way, cleanly with a needle, stick or scissors. On plaster, use wood or rubber because metal tools may scratch through to the plaster. If you slice only part of the way through the paper clay, you may snap the sections apart very cleanly later at leather or bone dry stage. Edges may be sponge rubbed or fettled smooth when the clay is bone dry.

Fold and roll your shapes when the clay is at the right dryness – too soon, and a soft slab will collapse, so be patient. Too late, and a stiff slab will crack. It is usually unnecessary to join or seal the ends of slabs with p'slip, while the slabs are still soft. When dry, they can be filled in without distorting the surface.

To drape soft slabs as clothing or covering, roll the paper clay out on water-repellent work surfaces to reduce moisture loss in the slab and retain pliancy work time. For the drape to hang correctly, the figure underneath should be in the right proportions.

A way to create volume with soft slabs is to fold and/or crimp slabs just after the leather stage of stiffness is attained. Water-absorbent work surfaces dry out the clay to this stage more quickly. Form and bend the cut-out shapes into freestanding three-dimensional hollow forms. Simple geometric shapes work well. When bone dry, the paper clay structures are strong enough to be handled without distortion. Most alteration, addition, trimming, carving and sealing with p'slip and paper clay will be easier over forms which are bone dry. Other possibilities with such shapes are discussed in the section on armatures in the next chapter.

Fragile window drape of paper clay is placed in position on a frame without distortion because it is bone dry. *Photographs by Rosette Gault.*

Leslie Lee works in progress – here a 'skirt' of paper clay has been contoured over bone dry figures. See finished work on p.12.

ABOVE; LEFT AND RIGHT Align cellulose fibre in a layer of p'slip by combing in one direction with fingers. For reinforced slabs or joins, oppose direction of 'grain' in multiple layers. Paper fibres are visible before firing, but burn out in kiln.
Photographs by Sue Hungerford and author.

When planning and designing new shapes, I make test shapes with folded paper cut-outs until I have the proportions right. Enlarging and reducing features on a photocopying machine will also help quickly and accurately size shapes and template outline patterns. Cut and save paper, cardboard, or vinyl shapes for those patterns you use most often. To cut exact multiples of a specific shape, stack two leather slabs on top of each other without water or slip in-between. Then cut the shape outline through both layers of clay simultaneously. Soft slabs may also be imprinted with a myriad of surface designs and textures before or after the cuts are made.

Making 'waves' from p'slip using a rib. The paper fibres are visible in the clay.

Soft strip construction

To create a versatile alternative to coils, measure and cut strips from softer flat slabs. These can be interwoven, or shaped as desired, or nested when soft. Assemble the dry strip shapes to build up structures at bone dry. Smear p'slip over the surface as adhesive. For example, dried oval outlines made from strips can be stacked on top of one another to make a volume. Another great use for cut strips is for reinforcement on the interiors of existing structures. Dipped in p'slip, they make excellent 'bandages'. For more information, see the sections on coil building, armatures or reinforcement.

Soft slabs: controlling, warping and clamshell effect

ABOVE Pinched figures by Ann Verdacourt (New Zealand).

Try to create and preserve a uniform and orderly arrangement of clay particles within the interior of the slab. This will be almost automatic with the poured p'slip over plaster method. Slabs of clay store information as a computer does; every time you move or twist a fresh soft slab you are in effect giving instructions to that slab like an invisible recording of your every touch. This 'recording' or, more accurately, changed alignment of

clay particles, may cause warping later when drying and firing, no matter how flat the slab appears initially.

To avoid warps when handling fresh soft slabs, I always try to balance the sequence of instructions to 'bend'. For example, if I have bent a slab in one direction 30° then I will deliberately bend it a second time in the opposite direction 30°. The two equal but opposing stresses neutralise the stress and reverse the conse-

Pulling up soft strips cut from p'slip slab.

quences of the bend. If I forget to bend the slab back before I flatten it, it may warp while drying. In general, the softer the paper clay is to start with, the less need to take this precaution.

Slab 'memory' can be controlled to advantage in some situations. For instance, to make the edges of the slab form to warp 'shut' like a clamshell or conversely to 'warp' open, pre-torque the slab in the desired direction. As the slab dries, it will tend to move exactly as intended, a subtle but powerful trick which is particularly useful for very thin porcelain work. See also the diagram on p.133 on how clay 'memory' works.

Rigid flat slabs and tiles

Even extra-large paper clay sheets may be dried flat in the open air on plaster. A base of a deflocculated slip recipe is to be preferred. Also, if the paper clay slab has reached bone dry flat, it is unlikely that it will warp further, especially if fired properly.

Spread a fairly thin 3–5 mm ($\frac{1}{8}$–$\frac{1}{4}$ in.) first layer of p'slip on the plaster, lift the 'soft leather' up just once from the plaster and rest it back down again on the plaster. This action will introduce a microscopic layer of air which will keep a large p'slip sheet from sticking to the plaster as the paper clay dries and shrinks. Smooth successive thick layers of p'slip over top. Begin surface treatment as desired. The layers can be uneven if the design requires it. Permit paper clay sheets to air-dry completely on a dry plaster slab, or possibly on a grill or open-air screen. As the air evaporates from the slab surface above, the plaster will continue to absorb moisture evenly from below. This drying process from below the slab continues even when the slab is leather-hard. Avoid the premature transfer of leatherhard tiles or slabs off the plaster to finish drying on a shelf.

Because most kilns, even electric ones, fire unevenly, avoid firing larger 'thin' slabs on edge without adequate support. I have flat fired 80 cm (32 in.) wide, thin, flat dried paper clay sheets, even ones with thick and thin areas ranging from 3 mm to 6.5 cm ($\frac{1}{8}$–$2\frac{1}{2}$ in.) thick, bridged over kiln shelves in an oval kiln. The kiln shelves were sprinkled with a small amount of sand to allow movement and shrinkage. I was careful not to exceed the temperature of slump for the parent clay.

Multiple layers and grain
Another feature of paper clay that can be controlled is the 'grain' (predominate directions) of the pulp fibres in a slab. Comb or rake through the wet p'slip, with your fingers in a consistent direction; this will cause the cellulose tubes to line up parallel to one another. You may alternate grain direction in successive layers as you wish.

Submarine by Jerry Caplan (USA).

Tile patterns by Arthur Huette (Canada).

Slab construction with bone hard shapes

Box construction with bone dry paper clay

Bone dry flat slabs are reminiscent of drywall. Wood construction, tools and joints are methods that can be employed. To cut the slabs when dry, score them with a needle and then snap them apart. Rub a wet sponge over dry edges to soften rough areas. A wood rasp tool may help plane the edges too. Wet the dry edge you are working on with water before using the rasp. Also, flat shapes and straight edges may be precut or partially cut during the soft or leather-hard condition. Snap flat shapes apart without distortion at the bone dry stage.

To make wet on dry box shapes:
1) Soak ends to be joined in water;
2) Assemble the bone dry flat edges, using the previously mentioned basic adhesion wet to dry;
3) Sponge water, score (if weight bearing), apply p'slip as adhesive and paper clay as putty in, around and over the wet fresh joint. See pp. 51–2 for more information about structural support and engineering considerations using reinforcement before firing, especially when walls are thin.

Notes

1 See notes on firing in Chapter 8.
2 See the information on clay recipes in Chapters 1 and 3.
3 See the Juvonen Report on p.122.
4 Specific maturing and water-tight temperatures for certain recipes of vitrified paper clay exist, though they are not common. The ash in cellulose tubes, which is a natural flux, self-glazes on the interior of the bodies at high temperatures.
5 See the Juvonen Report on p.122.
6 For industrial information, contact New Century Arts, listed in the Appendix.

Chapter Six

Large-Scale Sculpture

Scale up to life-size

By the time a work stands at 120 cm (48 in.) or more, a refined blend of paper clay and traditional building rules apply. Issues irrelevant to small-scale must be reckoned with when work is scaled up. The downward pull of gravity, support system, base weight, shrinkage and balance all become significant. Dimension of the available kiln, doorways, platforms, transport vehicles and shelving suddenly become more crucial.

This chapter examines various aspects of the construction process. Paper clay offers the opportunity at the bone dry stage to stabilise, refine, repair, cut, assemble, model new sections, improvise, and trim at intermittent dry/rewet/dry/rewet episodes. As you increase in scale, this practical and efficient feature proves to have immeasurable value.

Whether you add, subtract, build up with thin walls or carve down from thick chunks, the imagination of a sculptor is well served by the versatility of paper clay. Complex assembly forms are likely to survive and therefore become worth attempting.

Those who build by means of simple coil benefit too. No need to take extra time to score, for example. Instead, one can focus on graceful silhouettes, curves and arcs, occupied by the new structure in space. Bone dry is a better time to fill in the gaps, smooth out, and tend to the surface burnish between or over coil

lines. When the coils are hardened, the risk of distortion is minimal.

Consider open-air shrinkage an asset

At any size, all forms of pure clay shrink. A fraction of pulp inhibits the shrinkage a bit, but the 1% difference, in practice, is negligible. A life-size once-fired porcelain form moves downward and inward a handspan-width all the way around! Low-fired forms shrink too, albeit a bit less.

There are two 'start-to-finish' phases of shrinkage. The first occurs outside the kiln door in open air. In this phase, the contraction of the shape occurs in 'slow motion' as water evaporates. At bone dry, shrinkage pauses. Dried out paper clay remains 'as is' unless, or until, you decide what happens next. Leatherhard paper clay is still 'active' below the surface. As such, to assemble all parts at leatherhard is to work with shapes that are unstable compared to shapes at bone dry. The course of construction continues until the appearance of the sculpture satisfies in every detail. Then it is ready to load in a kiln. The second phase of shrinkage happens behind the kiln door. Neither hands nor tools will stop the shrinkage process during firing.

The good news is that phase one shrinkage (from wet to bone dry) mimics and informs the path of future shrinkage in the fire at phase two, so force greenware to dry. Do not cover in plastic. Let works move at random. Give them sun, warm kilns (do not exceed 100°C/212°F), and/or open air. Resist the urge to 'baby' works dry like you must do with conventional clay. Slow drying is counter-productive for paper clay.

Force-drying shrinkage shows up stress cracks likely to worsen in firing. See if or where the large clay form moved on its own. Note that any movement leans in the direction of least resistance. Plan to spot potential problems like weak areas, cracks, thin spots (etc.) at the bone dry state. Take all the time as you please to repair, thicken, reinforce, putty-in, seal or whatever is needed by wet-on-dry methods. The larger the scale, the greater investment of your resources, the more sense this procedure makes.

Tight seams survive fire

Consider use of a 'pre-bend' technique to insure a super secure join between very large slabs, coils or handles. To illustrate, an example with slab construction follows.

Cut two identical soft large slab shapes with a needle tool. Place each in separate but identical slump plaster molds. Bend edges of each soft side gently 'in' a few inches further than you actually want as soon you can handle the soft slab without fingerprints. Then, let each shell shape to air-dry in the curve you want. No one can see on the 'outside' the suggestion you made to the 'inside.' Now carry on again with assembly.

Adhere the two bone dry forms end to end with a seal of fresh paper clay/p'slip adhesive between them. When the seam dries without a crack, you know you added enough pulp to your clay for the project. If not, a few surface cracks may show. Fill them and add some extra pulp to the p'slip oatmeal to help. Next big batch, fine-tune the proportion of pulp

you prefer with the amount you need for bigger size. In general the bigger the work, the more pulp. More information on adaptations for sculpture base clays is given later on this chapter.

During the stress of high fire, gentle curls may begin that you induced in the slabs when they were soft. However, both slabs meet equal resistance at the join and so the seams tighten shut like a clamshell. All things being equal, if you were to over-fire such a seal, the walls would collapse before the seams opened. I've tested this many times with a variety of traditional and paper bearing porcelain. If you use the same method, but orient parts in reverse, expect seams and slabs to warp 'open' like magic. For the maker who desires to master the most difficult and unforgiving of clays such as porcelain and porcelain paper clay at large-scale, this expert technique can be key to great joins, confidence and a seamless result.

The value of working on bone dry

Intermittent work sessions on the bone dry structure give the sculptor a degree of control over the final outcome impossible to gain by other means. Most cut, trim and section procedures are more reliable at this stage. Pre-shrunk and fully bone hard assembly parts are more stable. Wire or mesh armatures serve no function. Bone dry clay supports just as well or better. Most joins bond right away and are strong enough to be pre-tested by hand. Practical advantages like these reduce risk and free the artist from the distraction of technical concerns.

Cut, trim and section at bone dry
To fit figurative paper clay sculpture in a kiln, it might make sense to divide the form up into several smaller shapes.

Any decision for 'cut lines' will be most clear at the point when the full form exists in space. View it from near, far, above, below or around all sides. The best places for cut lines follow along natural curve crease lines that least interfere with smooth contours. Arbitrary horizontal 'cut lines' contribute nothing of value to the majority of sculpture or tile ideas. If anything, most grid lines interfere with the overall image and appearance of a sculpture.

If you cut after the air set occurs, match-up between reinforced sections is quite stable and less likely to warp. Cut bone dry paper clay apart with any kind of power or handsaw. Through thick, dense areas, it may make sense to 'pre-score' the potential cut line(s) in advance. Just before the wet clay stiffens, scribe a guide line with a needle tool. Leave approximately 0.25 cm ($\frac{1}{8}$ in.) of the clay line intact. At bone hard the scribed line is a ready-made guide for the saw. If your shape permits, snap sections or tiles apart at bone dry. Straight score lines lend well to the snap method (see pictures on p.48).

For clean machine or power tool cuts in some high fibre clays and slabs, make a super-sharp blade cut through a temporary additional layer of gaffer tape or masking tape. It may help to sketch the intended saw path on the tape surface with a clear dark marker before you begin to cut. Remove the tape after. In some situations, super-crisp machine cuts are best done to a sinter rather than raw piece. The sinter fire method will be discussed in more detail in the section on carving down ultra-thick chunks of paper clay.

For many, the right 'cuts' will be a curve and not a straight line. However, sections probably won't free-stand and balance on their own in the kiln over a curve. To temporarily balance the section during firing, prop with a soft firebrick or improvise a bone dry 'nest' or 'scaffold' out of a large coil(s) of spare paper clay. You could also use or design a saggar. Remove all supports after firing.

To trim and tidy up before firing, wipe or rub edges smooth with a damp sponge. Do not wait till after fire for this step. Soft 'snips' turn razor sharp during firing. Then, only leather gloves may protect your skin from them. Plus special tools to sand, file or grind off the problem take time and effort to procure. Attention before firing is the easiest cure.

Seals on bone dry

Seals and joins between bone dry paper clay parts stick. The whole joint or work area undergoes a shrinkage and expansion process that is controlled by the presence of the hollow tubular fibres that wick water inside, between, around and through the clay. As a precaution for high load joints, pre-score and rough up contact surfaces for maximum adhesion.

Leatherhard stage paper clay pores remain too 'full' of water to induce the 'hidden velcro' kind of join. At leatherhard, a deep score procedure is a must. In general, the way the uniform slab or form dries out is exactly the way it will stay, unless the slab is overfired. The presence of paper fibre stabilises a flat tile shape if you handle carefully from the start. A common error is to move and handle leatherhard slabs as if they were bone dry and then wonder why a sudden warp appears.

Assembly technique for large-scale

When bone dry forms are too big to tack together with two hands, use belts of string or masking tape to hold the sections temporarily together. As a preliminary to the

Greenware 'castings' from plaster moulds (see opposite), waiting to be assembled. The strong greenware is held together with masking tape, keeping it in position while seams are joined together with wads of p'clay and thick p'slip.

Plaster/pulp (sandcast) forms, shown upright. The moulds can be laid flat and slabs slumped into them – the sand lends great texture to them and does not inhibit their drying out.

full seal process, wad in balls of putty-soft paper clay to join each form at five or more key points, curves or corners along the proposed seam line. Adjust the balance and placement of soft wads until the alignment is right.

At bone dry, remove the temporary belts of string or tape. By then, the new form may have moved off centre. Shimming up at the base is often the easiest cure. When joining wads are bone dry, seal in gaps and model with fresh soft paper clay putty. The form as a whole stands strong while you work and the risk of accident is less. Also the method reduces any danger of unintended torque on the big sections as you fill in and alter tight spots.

Reinforcing at bone dry

At bone dry again, determine whether the new form has turned top-heavy in the course of events. If so, reinforce and thicken areas below 'v' shapes and thin tube shapes. In a 122-cm (4-ft) vertical span of clay, this translates to a gentle taper of the wall thickness too. An easy method is to build the form with even walls first. At bone dry adhere a fresh soft slab, lattice or coil, dipped in p'slip, like bandages to the interior bottom half to reinforce or thicken. Layers and or cross-braces stabilise the form from within. Unlike pottery, substantial base weight can reduce the chance of tipping over.

It may be a good idea to apply a fresh paper clay soft coil along the inside of

69

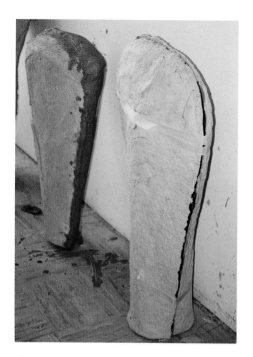

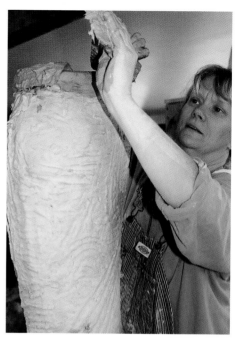

Greenware forms, one taped and not sealed. The form at the back has been sealed at the seams and will dry without cracks (provided enough pulp is in the recipe).

Both sides joined and force-dried at bone dry — now the 'lip' is finished with fresh layers of p'slip, coils and modelling.

the bottom edge. The coil is out of sight and it lends extra support and stability to the base during transport and fire.

Build for easy installation

Plan for final installation before firing or earlier. Plan for a generous interior hollow in the armatures to admit support tubes in case you require them. Holes drilled as a last minute after-thought in bone dry paper clay will: 1) shrink in diameter (if fired); 2) be limited to the diameter of the drill bit and torque power of the drill.

If you sectioned the form so it could be fired, reattach finished sections on site with a gasket of marine strength epoxy resin or silicone rubber. If flexible stability in wind or traffic is desired,

plan to mount big work as a 'sleeve' or 'cover.' Slip the form over a semi-flexible tube or post that has been countersunk down in the ground. In the event that the sculpture would ever be moved or taken down, it may make sense to put a second segment of plumbing tube inside your sculpture to make lifting up and off easy. If the installation is outdoors, allow enough flexible adhesive (like sili-cone gel) to allow for expansion and contraction in extreme temperature. Avoid trapping rainwater or snowmelt into 'enclosed' pools or big pockets by careless use of adhesive too. If the available space fills to the brim and turns to ice, the ice expands. The rigid clay walls may not be strong enough to resist the stress.

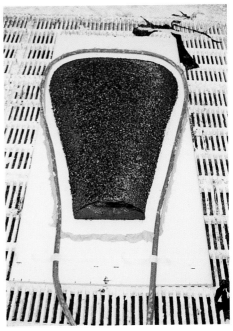

Dip soft slabs of paper clay in p'slip to use as bandage 'wrappings' over bone dry.

Pat down hump of wet sand into shape desired, then apply thick plaster. This was done on a formica-covered kitchen counter, so the plaster released easily.

Before firing
Secure bone dry 'tube' between inner/outer walls with soft paper clay putty as an adhesive.

After firing
Slide PVC tube into ready-fired 'hole'. Fix with waterproof silicone adhesive at intervals.

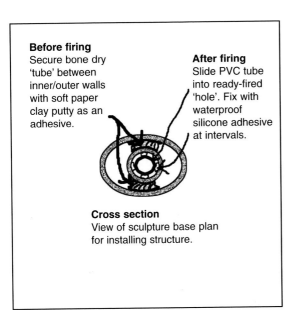

Cross section
View of sculpture base plan for installing structure.

To install
Fit sculpture form over post.

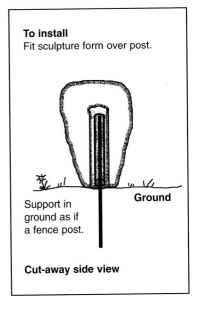

Support in ground as if a fence post.

Ground

Cut-away side view

71

Carving blocks of paper clay

Carving down a block of paper clay (see p.135 and p.48) lends itself well to certain paper clay recipes or combinations thereof. Paper clay as a carving medium has potential advantages over stone:
1) The sculptor gets to decide the ideal size, colour, texture, density, hardness, fired weight and composition of the 'chunk' before they begin to carve.
2) No trouble need be taken to hollow out the insides, particularly if you have enough pulp in the base mix. At the very start, poke a decent hole in your chunk of soft clay with a stick and turn the chunk over. When the chunk is dry, get started on the sculpture. Later when it is time to install the sculpture, you can decide whether you need the hole(s) you made earlier on, or not.

Force dry your chunk(s) for the early warning benefit explained earlier. If cracks show up, the cause and cure is the same as explained above. At this

point, decide whether to keep and carve through the fibres or get rid of them by means of a quick sinter fire.

If you keep the fibres, and carve on bone dry, rewet the work areas with a sponge as you go to help ease the resistance. Keep your tools sharp too. Power tools may be used with caution. Experienced sculptors have no problem with carving perfect detail on bone dry but those with less years of practice may not yet have the knack of the skill or the best shape of tool blade to get the effect they want.

Fortunately, it is easy to remove the fibres and a pleasure to carve without them (see picture p.135). Heat the chunk to sinter out the paper fibres. 570°–1000°C (1058°–1832°F) is hot enough to do the job and takes only a few hours. The result is a soft surface that resembles soapstone or soft plaster. The texture is smooth, and detail is impeccable, especially so with a fine-grained no-grog, no-sand base recipe of paper clay. Power tools can be used with caution. In the event of error on sinter or bisque, soak the affected area with water and rebuild fresh over top. If cracks develop, you can repair most, if not all of them using p'slip and coils of p'clay as discussed (see p.50).

Smearing p'slip into moulds results in perfect castings, as the plaster draws the clay particles to the surface leaving the fibres just below. This means the surface is a smooth cast while the fibres add strength.

P'slip castings of carved and altered plaster moulds are another avenue to explore. Here I have cut out the centre of my moulded shape, once the clay has firmed up a little.

RIGHT A force-drying experiment of a wet assembled form – with the kiln door open. Do not let this temperature go above 100°C (212°F).

Large-scale firing

To get the permanence, look and feel of ceramic clay and/or glaze, you really need to fire your work. The reward is a permanent aesthetic document built to last. The fired weight is less than the average traditional clay too as the paper burns out. There is no need for any metal or mesh armature. The translucent quality of high-fired porcelain becomes possible to achieve on a large scale. Almost all fired paper clays prove outdoor and weatherproof. Still, the firing process can be a drama in itself. As with normal glazing, the glaze colour you see before firing is not necessarily what you get after. Both traditional clays and paper clay resemble stone in that extreme or sharp shock is their greatest weakness.

Few kilns have perfectly even firing temperatures top to bottom. Hot spots and temperature variance of several cones (20°–50°C/68–122°F) are normal, no matter what the fuel. Free-standing forms

73

larger than 1 m (3.3 ft) often span the full vertical limit of the kiln. If the forms are not engineered to withstand uneven heating stress (i.e. wall thickness too thin for the height) as explained earlier, cracks and other problems can occur. The danger of slump or collapse increases as you approach the melting point of the base clay. Thin-walled porcelains are most vulnerable, followed by stoneware.

Be sure you have found the best firing temperature for the mix too. High temperature bisque, cone 03 or 04 is preferred. If not, high-fired stoneware or porcelain paperclay can be soft, and even crumbly at cone 08.

As a precaution with big porcelain structures, lower the temperature to about cone 8. Hot spots of cone 10 or more are likely in big kilns, no matter what the cone near the peephole says. Length of time and kiln atmosphere (reduction) can cause early fluxing too. When you reach an expert understanding of porcelain variables such as the structural mechanics for your specific shape, form of porcelain, skill level and kiln, you will know exactly how hot, how tall or how wide, how thick or thin you can go. To master firing, you must understand all phases between solid and fluid in large porcelains and the best moment to cut off the fuel.

Paper clay recipe composition

Add as much pulp to the base recipe as you can tolerate. A volume of 35–45% is more usual for large-scale. If it is impractical or too late to mix a new high-pulp batch, at least add extra pulp to the sealant/adhesive p'slip you use to make joins. Sufficient pulp to stop the show of drying cracks varies with the type of base clay used. For example, most earthenware ball-talc no-grog paper clay may require slightly less pulp than a high firing no-grog porcelain paper clay. If your base clay recipe was top-of-the-line potters' throwing stoneware, a bit less pulp may do. The actual percentage you settle on depends on variables of local pulp and regional clays impossible to predict with further accuracy than this.

Grog and sand used to be among the only correctional anti-shrink and leather-hard stabiliser additives to traditional sculpture clay. There is little to no reason to put these stabilisers and fillers in a paper clay. To avoid a rough texture and get a super-smooth perfect surface to carve on, omit grog and/or sand entirely.

If the texture of grit additive is part of your style and aesthetic, then cut the proportion back if you can. To create instant supertexture and reduce the fired weight to the minimum, consider a granular burnout material such as perlite in paper clay instead of grog. The 'mystery rock' surface, after firing, attracts interest and attention too. Whatever you choose to add or omit, do not let the total perlite/pulp blend added go too high, or you risk a crumbly result rather than a solid form. The same goes for total volume proportions of grog/sand/pulp.

Air-set sculpture

It may be that once you build, a kiln the right size becomes available. If not, air-set finish is a real possibility (i.e. allowed to simply dry rather than being fired). Air-set green paper clay is far less brittle than the same form in ceramic. WYSIWYG, or 'what you see is what you get' finish methods reduce the risks of further changes in size, colour, shape or weight. There is no size limit. Wax, paint, polyurethane, acrylic and oil all adhere well. Burnishing or polishing can also be done.

When you scale up with an air-set preference, do not overlook the good features of other plastic modelling media. Compared to paper clay, a concrete or ultra-dense plaster is quite heavy and requires an inner metal mesh armature to start on. So also does papier mâché. Many variations of not-for-kiln lightweight materials, plasticenes, plastics and foams exist and may also work well.

Clay habits to watch for

Some procedures for traditional clay do not transfer well to paper clay work. They are even counterproductive. Rethink the reason behind the habit before you decide which ones to keep. The force of the following habits took me a while to unlearn.

1) Why 'baby' newborn clay forms with soaking wet towels and wraps of plastic

One face mould can be used for many paper clay press-mouldings, and each one can be altered or modelled to change facial structure, gender and expression.

between work sessions? This habit blinds the sculptor from learning precisely where and what adjustments will be needed to succeed in fire.

2) Why bisque everything before glaze? Paper clay at bone dry is absorbent and can be dipped in glaze at bone dry and still hold its shape long enough for evaporation to occur. Bisque firing used to be the only way to make clay absorb enough water from the glaze to cause a uniform deposit of glaze on the surface without losing the shape.

3) Why assemble everything impatiently at the leatherhard stage? As explained, most large-scale leatherhard structures are in practice not as stable as they are at bone dry.

75

Wall Page by Ibrahim Wagh (UK), 40 × 50 × 1 cm (15¾ × 19¾ × ⅜ in.). Metal wires were laid on a slab surface in position before firing. After firing, dark areas remain.

Chapter Seven

Sculpture and Beyond

As a medium, paper clay can be supportive, responsive and expressive. Multiple work sessions provide opportunities for improvisation and imagination at every stage. Working knowledgeably with the natural flow of moisture in and out of paper clay can be supremely advantageous. Possibilities for paper clay as a sculptural medium extend beyond the basics into many areas.

In this chapter we will look at alternative directions and assembly methods now being explored.

Armatures for figures

It is now possible to design and make inner armature structures for larger sculptures out of bone dry paper clay parts or interlocking tubes. Much depends on the scale and complexity of the intended piece. Wire or metal support is not usually needed because paper clay as greenware is strong enough to support itself.

Potential armature sections can be made by coil, pinch, slab or hollowed out solid blocks. Any dry form can be used as a starting point. It is better if the form is hollow wherever practical. See discussions about wall thickness, air bubbles, clay shrinkage, reinforcement and firing for further clarification on this point.

Borrow techniques from the cement and plaster sculpture traditions for use with paper clay. Apply and embed paper clay and/or p'slip on a wire mesh or chicken wire structure. It is hard to believe, but a bone dry paper clay armature without chicken wire is likely to be just as strong as the bone dry wire armature would be. Test fire a sample first to see if this method will fire properly with your clay.

Basic shapes for armatures and support structures

Traditionally, a wire armature has been used to support a plasticene (oil-based) modelling clay for freestanding figures. The work in progress was kept covered in plastic to extend the work time. Modelling the soft plasticene could continue almost indefinitely. Conventional clay could not be used over wire, because these clays eventually shrink and crack as they dry. Also, conventional clays should be of a uniform wall thickness throughout which need not be the case with the plasticene figures. The wire armature/plasticene method is effective but it is a less versatile work surface than paper clay.

In ceramic studios, plastic coverings and wet towels were used to keep the clay soft for as long as possible. Newspaper stuffing or sand sacks and the like were used to support the structure during the modelling and were removed or emptied after modelling so that the piece could dry out evenly. Most conventional clay is too vulnerable when dry to be worked on.

Paper clay structures and figure parts can be made by hand or by plaster mould and left to dry. In fact, wet paper clay parts and joins can even be force or toast-dried when time is short. Wet soft layers of fill are moulded over the top of the strong dry structure.

Tube shapes for armatures

Lay out a group of bone dry tubes, hollow rolls, crimped in position to suggest a stick figure and torso. Let them stiffen to bone dry as leatherhard is not as strong. With water, p'slip and paper clay, assemble the parts into bundles that will become legs, arms, hands, feet, torso, shoulders, neck, etc. When these are dry and stiff, apply muscles and contours. Fill in the pockets with water, p'slip and paper clay. When these are dry, again with water, p'slip and paper clay, assemble your figure on its platform.

A simple and fast way to make a head or skull armature is to make two matching bone dry oval pinch pots, let them dry hard, and assemble them with water, p'slip and paper clay rim to rim. When this egg shape is bone dry, it can be dipped in water and p'slip and topped with a layer of soft paper clay for modelling the facial features. Cut an opening at the bottom of the head where the neck will be attached. Place it in position over the torso.

Much of the final surface detail and trim can be modelled, carved or even coloured on individual body parts before they are joined. Hard to reach areas can be given surface treatment texture and colour before assembly when appropriate.

Using templates and moulds

Experiment by cutting and folding various shapes out of soft slabs for torso and body parts. Variations on fabric patterns are alternative choices for the inner figure structures. Muscles and contour go on top of the bone dry 'clothes' in this case. Handle the folded shapes dry and determine the best sites for inner reinforcement at that time. More information on folding slabs was discussed in the previous chapter. Bone dry castings from a variety of moulds can be used to serve as the starting point for armatures also. Treat the castings as if they were tubes or folded shapes. The use of paper clay in moulds is discussed later on.

Armatures give strong support for details, such as these muscles added to bone dry armatures.

Rewet bone dry slab armature with water.

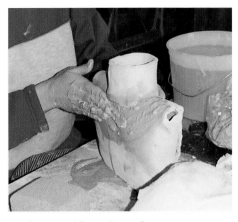

Apply some p'slip to the surface.

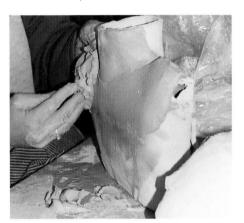

Putty in soft paper clay over armature.

Smooth over as needed into corners over the armature.

Apply more paper clay to contour the muscle, or texture the surface.

Adjust angle and position of bone dry mask to neck with wet paper clay and p'slip.

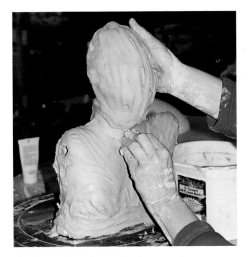

Apply a contour layer of soft paper clay as required.

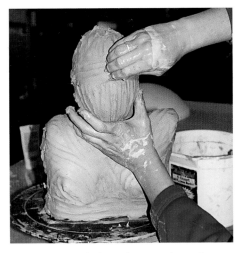

Make a texture in the soft paper clay surface as desired by hand (as shown) or tool.

LEFT Final assembly of head over neck. Note: detail on head was contoured before assembly. Artist: Kree Arvanitis (USA). *Photographs by Rosette Gault.*

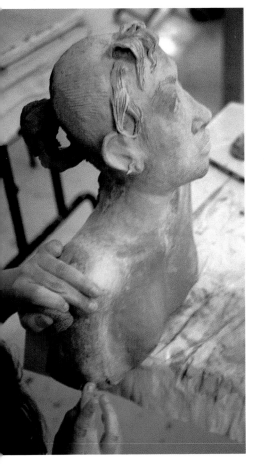

Unusual combinations

Dipping

A wide range of unusual and exotic forms and assemblages are now being tried with forms dipped in p'slip as the point of departure. You can dip organic forms such as tree branches, sponges, leaves, noodles, string, plants, birds' wings or bits of certain kinds of metal in a bucket of thick p'slip. You can even dip bone dry or bisque paper clay shapes.

Get a good coat, let it dry and then dip it several more times before assembly and firing. After firing (which could be extra smoky, not because of the paper burning off but because of the other material), a bisqued paper clay shell will remain. If the item were not dipped enough times, the 'shell' may be too fragile. My only caution is not to dip and fire plastic

Making paper clay armatures from a slab. P' clay is poured onto a plaster batt, and once it has set and is no longer a slurry, the edges can be prised up, and the slab removed. P'clay slices will bend easily.

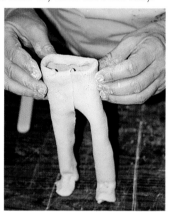

LEFT Cut out patterns using a wooden stick. CENTRE Fold and curl the pant form to create legs. RIGHT The hollow legs can be stood up and shaped into a position.

LEFT Fold the 'shirt' template into shape. CENTRE Form the shirt into a torso form by pinching it together, to form an armature. RIGHT Manipulate the form until satisfied. Muscles, details or clothes can now be added.

82

things because noxious fumes from the
plastics may be produced in the kiln area
during the firing.

Embedding ceramic pieces in p'slip

Try embedding ceramic cast or modelled
forms, bone dry greenware, bisque or
even glazed fragments in a bed of p'slip,
up to 7.5 cm (3 in.) thick of a high-pulp
mix if your idea requires it. I have
embedded small items, no bigger than
fit in my hand, directly into the wet,
high-pulp p'slip, let them dry and fired
them intact. Do not fire over the temperature rating for the previously glazed
ware unless distortions are desired.

Metals and glass with paper clay

Certain metals can withstand kiln firing
temperatures, and these too can also be
inserted into paper clay and p'slip. In
cases where the firing melts or vaporises
the metal, a greenish-black mark or halo
will result. See also the discussion under
armatures and surface treatments for
more uses of paper clay with metals.
Many paper clays, in fact, bond to metal.
The lignins in the cellulose have an affinity for the metallic oxides as well as clay
minerals. Dean Goss, at the East Carolina
University, worked out some precise p'slip
recipes which bond to metals at cone
04–05, some of which are listed on p.134.
P'slip, smeared over stainless steel and
fired can give distinctive surface textures

This llama figure, assembled wet on dry and
originally designed as an armature, is an inspiration for further variations on the theme.

Installation by Linda Heisse. String has been dipped in paper clay. The slip and burnt-out shell structure remains. RIGHT Detail of above.

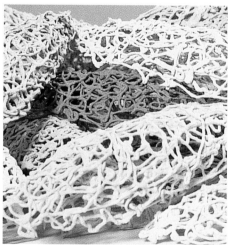

to the stainless steel.[2] Glass slumping in paper clays is another area starting to be explored by paper clay artists. Another potential use for glass is to insert colourful glass chips or batch (ground glass), beads or marbles into paper clays. These will melt in the pockets provided, though they may drip or leak out of vertical surfaces during firing. Test first.

Assemblage, collage, print

Assemble bone dry and/or soft greenware shapes or torn sheets or scraps into collage forms and/or figures. Use p'slip as the adhesive and generously rewet the area to be joined. Integrate or alter the form or image on the paper clay surface as part of the composition. Then subtract, carve or trim the work. Use the general guidelines for working with bone dry to wet paper clays. You can even repair bisque and incorporate bisque into the assemblage if necessary.

One bonus of waiting until the end for final assembly is that you can do the surface texture and colouration, even glazing on the individual bone dry parts before assembly. Then the borderlines can be very crisp between colours. Printing on paper clays will be discussed in the next chapter.

84

Moulds and casting

Plaster moulds

With paper clay, moulds are superb points of departure. Each paper clay casting can be customised with undercuts and surface carving to look in sharp focus with crisp detail *or* additive methods on dry castings can be used. With paper clay there is no technical reason for the artist to rely on a mould as the end point, as it might have been in years past. Assemblage of castings from moulds, as greenware, is another rich area of potential.

Plaster moulds serve as points of departure

Rather than finish with a plaster or latex mould, begin with one. As seen in the photo on p.43, p'slip can be smeared or poured directly over plaster. The casting detail is perfect because the absorbent plaster immediately brings all tiny clay particles to the surface, leaving the fibres just below. Pullout is easier too at leathersoft because of the fibre. Trim edges with scissors or needle tool and sponge.

In the photo on p.73 one can alter the casting and even the original commercial mould. Note the hand carving of pattern texture on columns and roof, which was made on the plaster before the casting was taken. The photo on p.75 shows a dramatic wet over bone dry 'makeover' of features to a standard cast classic goddess face – including new cheekbones, bone structure, lips, nose, eyes and hairdo. Use a face mould to save time – then change each to sculpt

RIGHT Peeling freshly set p'slip impression off an opened up plaster slipcast mould.

or carve a fresh personality over the cast. Please 'wake up the eyes' – there are enough ceramic death masks with empty eyes shut left over from the old days (before we understood paper clay) hanging around to last humanity at least a thousand years!

If you imagine it, nothing technical about paper clay stops you from adding the rest of the skull, neck or torso to the bone hard cast face, or vice versa. The series of photos on pp.80–81 show more details on torso armature assembly.

Paper/plaster moulds for large scale

A modest amount of pulp in plaster mixtures lends some strength to large-scale moulds. Measure the proper volume of room temperature water for your batch and measure the dry plaster in a seperate bucket as normal. Disperse handfuls of wet pulp into the measured amount of water and stir, then sift the plaster into the water. As usual, small 'islands'

ABOVE *Requiem* by Jim Etzkorn (Canada), width: 50 cm (19¾ in.). Multiple layers of string soaked in p'slip are set up in a plaster mould as part of an early stage of construction. *Photograph by D. Lee.*

BELOW *Book by Anna Ailincai (Canada), porcelain.*

Eggtray by Ann Verdacourt (New Zealand). Courtesy of the Dowse Art Museum, New Zealand. Earthenware eggs, paper clay stoneware tray.

show above the water line. Stir and mix as usual.

The more pulp that is dispersed into the measured water, the less 'room' there is for plaster. The more leftover plaster you have, the lighter the weight after the plaster sets up. While less weight is clearly an advantage for a life-size 'shell' of plaster, too little plaster equals an airy 'mould' that is too soft and crumbly to do its job. In the end, a little pulp helps, a lot can hinder.

Press-moulds/bisque moulds

Press-mould pliant paper clay as you would conventional clay into concave plaster, bisque or even plastic forms. Success will depend on the amount of moisture in the paper clay and the pressure you use.

Do not use any p'slip in or on bisque moulds because it adheres too easily to the bisque. Plaster is the easiest release surface for p'slip when the p'slip is leatherhard. If you must use a bisque mould with p'slip, place a layer of tissue paper between the bisque mould and the p'slip. Remove or fire away the paper after the p'slip has hardened.

Slipcast moulds

Slipcasting-type moulds respond well to all forms of paper clay slips. Studio-made p'slip should be poured or smeared into the slip moulds opened up. Castings set up quickly can be pulled or peeled out of the mould with minimal tearing just before leather-hard. Cast parts may be assembled and altered in 1001 possible combinations with wet on dry capability used to full advantage. However, only the commercial brand of Casting P'slip™ can pour smoothly into the moulds closed up the conventional way.

Peel rubber latex mould with texture off a bone dry p'slip casting. The texture for the latex mould was taken from a crusty sea rock. Undercuts are possible with this method of casting. *Photograph courtesy of Stephanie Snyder (USA).*

Latex rubber moulds

The best feature of castings from soft latex moulds is that they can have undercuts, unlike plaster, and are light-weight. Pour, smear or brush layers of p'slip into concave or convex latex. With all the undercuts, just be sure to wait until beyond the leatherhard or even bone dry stages before peeling the rubber latex off the cast form. Speed drying helps accelerate the process. Even so, alter the casting, add detail and trim before firing. The versatility of both paper clay and latex are well-suited.

Sand casting

Paper clays are ideal for forming under or over shapes of sand or fine gravel. There are several choice points and vari-ations that work well. One decision will be whether to build a hump of wet sand or dig out an open hollow in a bucket or a sandbox or even a beach!

If you build a hump of wet (sticky) sand, take time to pat down a smooth contour and keep the sand from drying out. To get a perfect shape at the bottom of the hump, it may help to measure and cut out a template for the bottom in cardboard or plastic in advance. Then pile up wet sand over the top of the tem-plate and keep the guide edge in view at all times. With hump shapes, it can help to imagine what the shell cast of paper clay will look like if turned upside down and/or inside out when it is pulled up from the hump. Hump moulds are a bit more tech-nical and time-consuming than the hollow moulds because you have to keep an eye on them from start to finish. The sand in the hump has to be soaked more often to keep it wet too. Also the shell of paper clay is best pulled off before leather-hard and should be set with care so as not to torque the 'lip-edge.' In time the cast will finish shrinking and attain a bone dry cured state. (See also the photos of cast plaster/pulp shells on p.69.) See a finished sand-cast work by Karen Hvsabo of Copenhagen Denmark on p.94.

Hollowed out sand-cast shapes are not so fussy. The paper clay you cast can, and probably should, stay in the mould until bone dry. Pat, tap down and smooth a good-looking hole of wet sand in a bucket, sandbox or beach. Again, imagine the cast shape will be turned upside down in the end.

The only other decision is whether to cast thick oatmeal p'slip 'as is' or whether to make the p'slip into a soft slab and press or drape the slabs/sheets in or over the sand. Soft slab has many advantages. One is that the cast dries faster. The second is the walls of the cast are automatically more uniform. The sacrifice is that the sandy surface texture may not pick up, and potential surface crinkles may not please. On a paper clay

piece, however, these can always be corrected. But you may not want to take the extra time, or may not have the patience and skill to correct the surface texture.

The other choice is to make a direct pour of thick p'slip. If you pour in a hollow, be prepared to scoop out the extra pools in the bottom. Be prepared for a series of multiple pours. High humidity in the air can increase the setting time by days. Pouring straight out of the bucket over a hump of sand is risky. It is likely the pressure of the falling stream of p'slip will dent the contour of the soft wet sand. Apply palmfuls of really thick p'slip one by one from the bottom up as an option.

Splatter and even stipple methods may suit you too. Abundant and variegated textures result.

The rest of the procedure is as normal for paper clays. Sand-cast paper clay shapes can be freeform and casual indeed. Suppose you make sand moulds on a beach in bright sun and/or breeze. Assuming the tide doesn't come in, the shapes dry out fast! Bone dry cast shapes can be stood on end, balanced upon one another to amuse and please the eye. Good pairs

can be joined at the seam. Assemble as many ideas and combinations as you have time for. Walk around, through and even under them. Drag them around. Take them apart. Put some back together. How high could you stack them? Try some as giant sand crayons. Nothing stays permanent until you really want it so. Recycle or resculpt over the shapes that flunk. The 'keepers' will be strong enough to carry and load in the back of your wagon or truck for firing or further refinement.

Maybe you live somewhere, like the Northwest of North America, where salt-soaked beach timber is a ready and tempting fuel. Bone dry clay is a good excuse to build a good hot and salty bonfire in and around the works onsite. Next morning, the tide will have come in and cleared the sand. In the ash of the fire pit, chances are extremely good to find fired clay in shapes of wonder and beauty.

Large-scale plaster moulds by sand-cast method

Large-scale sculptors who need or want to have giant plaster moulds for their paper clay can soon find a practical and easy method to prepare them. Build a hump or slump with wet sand over a board. Select

LEFT *Stranger in the Night,* a collaboration between Lily Bakoyiannis (Greece) and Garry Williams (Canada) at the Canada-Greece Ceramic symposium, 1996, height:183cm (6 ft). *For the first time ever I was able to make in clay some incredibly fragile and complex shapes such as slender twigs and branches ... when I opened the kiln I was astonished to see that bisque branches had successfully adhered to the greenware base... paper clay provides an aesthetic and technical freedom never before enjoyed in ceramic sculpture. Photograph by D. Lee.*

RIGHT *White Tower* by Melissa Floyd (New Zealand), cast paper clay and fired standing.

boards or door blanks with smooth water-resistant flat clean surfaces. Use sand or fine gravel as detailed in the earlier section on sand-cast paper clay.

Use thickened plaster instead of paper clay to cover the moist sand hump or open hole. After the plaster hardens on a hump, gently slide the new mould sideways a few inches or so. If you have a smooth surface, the lip of plaster will release and the pile of sand underneath will give way, allowing you safely to pry the new mould up.

Embedded sand lends a good texture to the surface of the plaster. The presence of leftover embedded pieces of gravel in the plaster will not stop absorbency of the plaster below. Drape slabs of paper clay into the plaster mould forms as most paper clay shapes dry out evenly on them. Most release at bone dry from the mould easily, despite the sandy-looking plaster surface. The rough texture imprinted on the surface of the paper clay form eases the process of assembly and alteration between multiple bone dry shells and shapes.

If you don't like the texture, but like the basic shape, start to scrape, carve and sculpt whatever surface you like through the sand as soon as the plaster has set up and you release it from the sand pile. When the mould itself is fully dry, after a week or so, so be it.

Those new to clay or plaster procedures may refer to the Appendix or the further reading list. Volumes have been written about the basics.

Large-scale works

The limit of your sculptures will be the size of the kiln or truck! More freedom to handle and transport greenware is another good reason to use paper clay for the larger-scale commission. Paper clays with large quantities of pulp are recommended for larger-scale works. Mix an open, high-pulp batch for the interior armature. This may be blended with a more medium-pulp mix for the outer shell. High and low-pulp paper clay of the same base are compatible. Pulp can be mixed in castable refractories also.

Air or force-dry the parts as you go. This avoids ultrawet areas on the interior which take ages to dry if sealed up. Do not be afraid of watering down the bone dry armatures multiple times as you build up. Bone dry parts that are dipped in water usually dry out again rapidly, more rapidly than they would as a wet or even leatherhard piece. Review the notes on construction, reinforcement and firing preparation given earlier in this chapter and the next. Gain a thorough understanding of your paper clay recipe, your glaze and firing limits by test firing well in advance of the project whenever feasible.

People ask about outdoor sculpture, and whether paper clays can withstand freezing after firing. This depends on the nature of the parent clay. See the notes on clay bodies earlier in the text for assistance on this. A good earthenware, energy-efficient clay recipe for outdoors was offered. More information about large-scale work will be mentioned in Chapter 8.

Notes

1 Dean Goss research with Dick Spiller, East Carolina University School of Art, Greenville, NC USA. 1992 (unpublished).
2 Glenys Marshall Inman and Nikos Slavenitis, Canada-Greece Symposium, Banff, 1996, have good results from experiments firing p'slips and glazes over stainless steel.

Chapter Eight

Surfaces and Firing

This chapter features surfaces, glazes and colours intended to be permanently fired and fused with paper clay. The surface textures and the colour possibilities for paper clay are nearly infinite. One could work the surface at any stage of the process – leatherhard, bone dry and greenware, bisque, and even overglaze lustres and china colours. Familiar glazes, engobes and slips can be used or new ones developed. Also, a wide

variety of non-fired colours such as acrylic paints, stains, oils, waxes, etc. can be applied to fired paper clay surfaces.

Any ceramic clay can be adapted to a coloured slip. Coloured slips can be used at all the different firing temperatures, and on nearly every clay. The palette can have as few as two and as many as 200 or more possible colour combinations. The artist who is venturing into the ceramic medium for the first time will have a solid point of departure on which to add variations and experiments.

Conventional glaze technology is equally suitable for use on paper clay.

The author loading p'clay porcelian structures into the kiln. The interior of each contains a glazed figures fixed in position (wet to dry) before the sides.

ABOVE Sand-cast piece by Karen Hvsabo (DK).

BELOW Burnished paper clay form by Merja Hellsten (Finland/USA/Germany), 1993. *When I switch countries and clay bodies, the transition to the new clay is easier with paper clay.*

If you would rather not make up your own slip substitute, store-bought underglazes rated to the same temperature as your clay are available. Glazes too can be purchased ready-made, but brands do differ, so I recommend buying small quantities of the leading candidates. Test fire them on your paper clay. Brush stripes of the underglaze colour you hope to use underneath. You will notice each clear glaze does something different to the colours of the ceramic oxide. This is information you need to have to feel more confident with colour. Select the clear glaze which best suits your need. Everything applied to surfaces before the first firing is likely to change colour, and possibly melt during each firing. So, when applying colour, what you see is not usually what you get until the firing is over. Test firing will help you to understand this better.

Slips and engobes

Slips can be thick or thin, or any stage in between. Slips may or may not have paper in them. A slip is best made from a base similar to that of the base of the paper clay you are using. Slips can be brushed on, sponged or even dipped. Slips when applied thick are opaque colour. Slips when thin are semi-transparent. Most slips by themselves have an open matt surface to match the source clay. I mix 10–20% by volume clear glaze in white slip as an all-purpose base. If you want more 'melt', add more clear glaze directly to the slip.

Clay surfaces are either shiny, satin matt or matt. The shiny surface can be an all-purpose transparent clear glaze. This leaves two remaining categories: satin matt and matt. Matt, or non-shiny, is the same as the clay surface. To make a set of coloured slips or underglazes, refer to p.126 for directions.

The *Dragon* paper clay kiln with pots in its belly breathed fire and smoke during the firing. Mike McCullough and workshop participants in Oahu, Hawaii.

I have about 12 colours of selected stains mixed with slip base that melt matt. At greenware, the surface of matt coloured slips or underglazes can be built up in layers, carved through, scraped off, textured, screened on, sprayed on, burnished, etc. After sintering, more colour can be applied or carving done, or you can skip the sinter temperature and go directly to bisque. At bisque, with the matt surfaces now set but open and porous, I can apply a thin wash of dilute colour, or touch up, or rub in more slip. All of this allows me to express what I want for the clay in use. I can always rebisque to build up more colours or even cover up colours that were unsuccessful. When satisfied, apply

95

the final glaze and fire. The final firing sets every colour permanently. At high temperatures, these earthenware slips melt a satin matt; at low temperatures, they melt matt. If there is clear glaze on the top, the surface should be glossy.

Textures and finishes

Slips can be built up thick with successive brush strokes to make opaque and rough textures on paper clay. Second layers of thin watercolour wash of the same slip can be used over or under the texture as highlighting. Slips can be many colours carved in and on and through to reveal the clay layer below.

Texture can also be made by paddling

stiff brushes, or pressing textured surfaces into the soft paper clay. In hard paper clay, texture can be scraped in or over with abrasive or stiff brushlike tools, forks or needles. Sponges and fan brushes are excellent for applying and building up texture too. Besides building up layers of non-paper bearing slips, p'slips will make a nice, if fibrous texture.

P'slip can be smeared on paper clay forms in any condition, even on wet bisque, and can be used in layers to build an interesting surface. It could even be smeared on conventional clay at leatherhard or before. Unusual textures ranging from paper to oatmeal to pastelike icing can be achieved depending on the thickness of the slip. Smear pastelike layers of p'slip to reinforce bone dry joints, to fill in pockets, or to assemble multiple bone dry parts. Alternate the grain of each successive layer if desired.

Close-up of Carol Gaskin and Peter Berry (USA) collaborative. Ceramic oxides have been airbrushed over the slab relief. Height (each tile): 81cm (32in.).

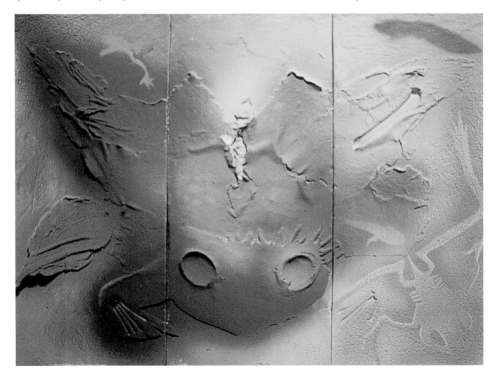

Fired paper clay wall work with silk screen printing by Maarit Makela (Finland).

Slips and terra sigillatas

Terra sigillata gives excellent results over paper clays. Terra sigillata slips are made of the very smallest clay particles. For surface decoration, these refined slips are brushed or sprayed thinly over the clay. The surface can be rubbed or burnished to a natural sheen.

Burnishing and smoothing

Paper clay can be smoothed with a flexible rubber rib or with your finger while the clay is still fairly soft. But don't compress the clay surface in this way if you know you are going to be adding successive layers of wet over dry because you will have to rough or scratch up the smoothed or burnished surfaces again to get good adhesion. When the paper clay surface is rubbed smooth with the back of a spoon or rock, it will compress the small particles on the surface and get shiny and a little dark. This is called burnishing but most burnishing doesn't stay 'shiny' throughout all the firing temperatures. To take the burnish out of the surface, carve it away with a fettle tool, or rewet it and rub with a sponge. If the clay is leatherhard and you want to smooth the surface, vigorously rub the bone dry surface with a damp or wet sponge and/or in combination with p'slip and/or slip. Burnishing is a traditional way to seal a clay surface without the use of glaze.

Silk screen glaze is transferred directly onto soft paper clay. The soft slab with image will be pliant for further alteration thereafter.

Tissue transfers guideline of ink from felt tip pen to fresh paper clay slab. Tissues can also be soaked with slips and oxides before transfer to clay surface.

Stamping, imprinting, silk screen

Paper clay takes textures and stamps quite well, and these can be altered with wet on dry if desired. Press stamps for impressions into as moist a paper clay as possible for best results. An exception is copperplate which will stick unless the paper clay is nearly dry according to one report (Isoniemi report from Finland). Stamps can be of all types – bisque, latex, metal, plaster, even dry paper clay. Sometimes it is advisable to lightly dust non-absorbent surfaces with talc or flour to affect a good release on the softer paper clay.

Imprinting or even silk screening can be done as a texture on leather sheets, and the leather sheets may then be rolled or folded into a different shape afterwards. With paper clay, the artist can continue to work or model over the bone dry images, perhaps to sculpt relief or highlight certain parts of the image in a way that could not be done with conventional clay.

Tissue transfer prints of pigments and/or ceramic oxides are also possible on flat or soft slabs which can then be folded and manipulated. Multiples of images can also be done, each one interpreted a different way with the original print as a point of departure.

One-fire glazing

One-fire glazes are easily added to paper clays, either on top of or incorporated into the slip. The fibres in the bone dry paper clay absorb the water glaze and the greenware is strong enough to resist deterioration when it is dipped, provided the walls of the dipped objects aren't paper-thin. Multiple dipping is possible provided you allow the walls to dry in-between. Note: thin walls of greenware paper clay do soften in water.

Multiple-fire glazing

Apply glaze to bisque paper clay the same as for non-paper clay. Whether you choose to brush, dip or spray, correct application will be the key. Sinter fire those glazes which are too crumbly to handle in preparation for multiple layers of glaze and/or wax resist techniques. Lustres and china paints can also be applied as overglazes.

Firing guidelines

All paper clays should be fired in well-ventilated areas and kilns. A kiln vent system, if functioning well, will make a big difference. There is a noticeable smoking period in the first few hours of the firing. The smell is like burning paper, especially if you have a lot of paper clay in your kiln. The smoking period will stop soon after about 250°C (451°F). If you have less paper clay in the kiln, you may not even notice the smell. Ceramic clays, even without paper, emit potentially toxic fumes, sulfides and such, later on during the firing process which are invisible and have no smell. Kiln vents should already be standard equipment in your studio. If not, get a large fan by a window and use it, especially at the early stages of the firing.

Trapped air bubbles within paper clay are not a problem in the firing provided the following guidelines are met:

1) The clay wall in any one place is not too thick for the pulp content (less than about 2.5–3.5 cm (1½ in.) for low-pulp, about 6 cm (2½ in.) thick for medium-pulp recipes, about 9 cm (3½ in.) thick maximum for higher pulp-bearing paper clays.[1])

2) The piece is sufficiently dry on the inside. Then steam inside will be able to escape out of the tubular network in the clay to the surface.

3) The piece is heated slowly at the beginning of the firing, especially from room temperature to boiling point of water.

Cup # 5, Ed Bamiling, (Canada).

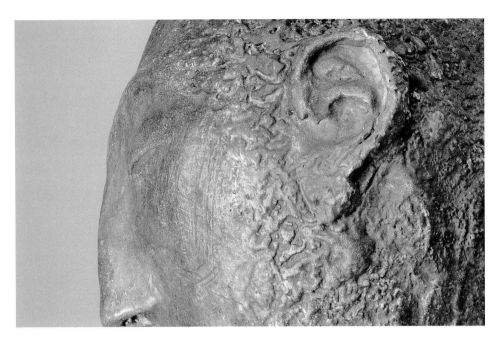

ABOVE *Textured Head* by Rosette Gault (USA).
Photograph by R. Shreiber.

LEFT *Painting with Glaze* by Glenys Marshall Inman (Canada). Porcelain paper clay fired to 1250°C (2282°F).

RIGHT Lighthouse by Rosette Gault (USA). The watery look is achieved with ultra thick p'slip. Height: 30 cm (11¾ in.). *Photograph by R. Schreiber.*

Bisque firing

Paper clays in general should be bisque fired much higher than normal, especially if they are based on stoneware, porcelain or high-fire clays, or if the pulp content is high. Fire at least to 1000°C/ 1832°F. If the bisque batch is quite fragile or even crumbly (due to high-pulp content), just refire to an even hotter temperature. Often paper which you might have recycled for the pulp has a lot of clay in it, which would increase the refractory quality of the overall clay recipe.

101

ABOVE Wall tiles, 15 × 15 cm each imprinted with photographic transfer prints by Linda Stanier (Canada). *Paper clay has been just great for pouring the thin slabs that I wanted for developing the photos, but the biggest bonus was the green strength and being able to sandblast my greenware.*

Ben Yang (USA) smears a thick layer of custom paper clay slip over a conventional coil form.

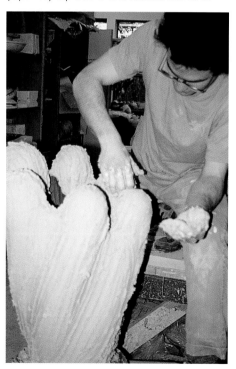

Glaze firing and raku

Firing of most paper clay should be to the normal temperature for the maturity of the paper clay. Almost any clay can be a raku clay when it has paper in it, even clays notoriously poor for raku such as porcelains and earthenware talc bodies. One-fire glazing of greenware paper clay is normally successful.

Paper clay 'kilns'

A discussion of paper clay would not be complete without mentioning that paper clays can be used for kilns and as kilns. Some structures are temporary, others are more permanent. Pulp, as mentioned, can be mixed with castable refractories for this purpose. Paper clay mixtures can be applied over themselves, wood or wire and wire mesh structures.

For temporary 'paper' kilns, sheets of high clay-containing papers such as the *National Geographic* can be dipped whole, not as a pulp, into buckets of slip and pasted on in layers over a frame to enclose and seal a load of pots. After firing, the paper clay shell is lifted off or is broken apart to reveal the finished ware. A whimsical variation on this theme was contributed by Mike

Tree by Rosette Gault (USA). Fingerpainting in thick p'slip.

This piece was fired flat bridged over kiln shelves even though it is 82 cm (32½ in.) long.

ABOVE *Stool* by Hanne Marie Beth Anderson (Italy/ Denmark), majolica. *For me it has been absolutely perfect. The legs could 'carry' much more and they are even so strong that one can sit on them.*

McCullough, who participated in an unusual project in Hawaii that included building and firing a paper clay kiln in the shape of a dragon. A chicken wire armature was made that held the pots in the belly. This dragon was stoked under its tail and breathed smoke and fire out of its jaws (see p.95).

Paper clays can stand a dramatic above-ground fire such as the 'castle' structure that was erected in Belgium in 1996 by Patty Wouters. Wood and combustibles were placed around the paper clay castle before it was draped with slip soaked paper sheets to seal. After firing, the ash was swept away, and the 'castle' was permanently fired.

Notes

1 Solid blocks of any high pulp clay up to 15 cm (6 in.) thick have survived firings, but test with your clay first. High pulp is necessary.

Chapter Nine

Further Developments

At this point we have highlighted the historical, technical and practical application and potential of paper clay. The aesthetic side of paper clay is, of course, both the end and the beginning of this book, depending on your point of view. Almost every area of ceramic form making whether sculpture, handbuilding, moulding or throwing has been touched, yet there is still room for advance. A shift to paper clay extends the possibilities for inspiration in surprising ways.

Paper clay for the wall

Paperlike sheets of paper clay were a natural starting point for many artists who have worked with paper clay, particularly since the Second World War.

These artists have replaced pigments and ink with ceramic oxides, stains, engobes and glazes which can withstand the firing. All manner of printmaking, pattern, image screening and surfaces have been used to fulfil their artistic visions.

Now such things exist as a sculptural 'painting'. Fully-fired ceramic sculptures can be embedded into the ultra thick surface of a paperlike sheet of paper clay, which is then fired multiple times until permanent. Very tactile finger painting directly on large sheets of ceramic paper clay was not possible before either. Also, paper clay can mimic paper,

Locked and Unlocked by Les Manning (Canada), 40 × 100 cm (15¾ × 39½ in.). *Photograph by D. Lee.*

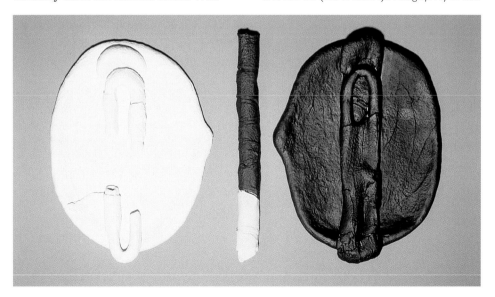

ABOVE Detail of installation by Nancy Selvin (USA). Paper clay castings with xerox transfers.

RIGHT TOP *With my Wishes* by Nikos Slavenitis (Greece). Installation for Canada-Greece Exchange Symposium, Banff, 1996. *Photograph by G. Marshall-Inman.*

RIGHT *Sueno,* by Laura Rosette (Mexico), 20 × 15 × 12.5cm (8 × 6 × 5 in.), earthenware.

cardboard, vinyl, leather and watery surfaces to perfection. Works such as 'glaze paintings' on the corrugated cardboard paper clay of Klaus Steindlmuller provoke an effective form of visual dissonance. How can this be a shiny rocklike clay and glaze when it looks so much like paper? The urge to touch this work is strong. Tactile, highly paperlike work by Mike Kusnick of West Australia (via the Czech Republic) would be another example. And there are considerable advances with imprinting and photo transfer techniques too as Paul Scott and others have shown. I have seen a lot of excellent work in the genre and I expect we will be seeing even more in years to come. It is clearly worth the extra time for detail and glaze work for artists when the chance of loss is less.

Freestanding and installation work

Freestanding works are an area in which the early results range from conservative to cutting edge. Towers and columns made of paper clay may look as if they are of conventional clay. When you transport them you discover they weigh less than you expected. The enormous,

ultra-thin porcelain bowl forms in paper clay of Leena Juvonen (Finland) serve as a three-dimensional canvas for painting with vibrant glaze colours. These have to be seen in person to be believed.

Greg Payce from Canada has been experimenting with a method that shows great promise. For his 'otherworldly forms', Payce suspends a small 5–7.5 cm (2–3 in.) abstract coil-built shape in midair. He then builds up the form from the inside out with ever more dry coil rings slathered in p'slip until the work grows – often to at least 46 cm (18 in.) in all directions. To try to see inside such a structure is to peer into pure mystery, imagination and labyrinth.

Nina Hole in Denmark uses a combination of fireclay with grog and pulp to

construct large outdoor structures and gateways, which she then wraps with kaowool and fires. She builds a large fire with wood inside the 'house' form. The opening at the top of the piece is the flue where the flames escape. When the 'house' reaches temperature, she stops stoking the fire and unwraps the kaowool to reveal the glowing hot paper clay. She says the presence of pulp helps with the thermal shock and also it is as strong as greenware for transport. This work is both an event and a finished structure: metamorphosis in every sense of the word.

Even large-scale works are being accomplished such as the *Brickyard Angel* just completed by Dave Porter at the Archie Bray Foundation for Ceramics in Helena, Montana, USA (see p.42 and p.110). This multiple-part paper clay figure was carved down with power saws to smaller kiln-sized 'blocks'. The blocks were reassembled with cement and mortar after firing.

Wall murals too, are now being made with paper clays. To make *Pneumatos*, a commission for Pacific Testing Laboratories in Seattle, WA, USA, Peter Berry and Carol Gaskin poured a huge 'pool' of p'slip in a wood frame over a bed of plaster drywall on a cement floor. Kiln-size pieces were cut out of the huge 'tile'. Birds' wings were dipped in p'slip and incorporated into the design which was saggar-fired.

The use of unfired paper clay is also becoming more common among some ceramicists. Many installation artists prefer to 'recycle' the paper clay after the photograph is taken and the show comes down, not unlike the ancient tradition of clay maché mentioned in the Introduction. Green strength makes transport and installation practical.

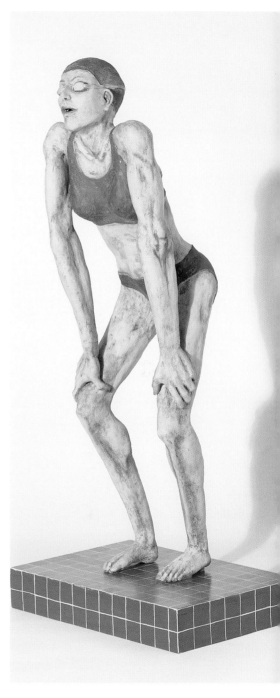

Untitled by Carmen Lang, 75 × 43 × 25.5 cm (29½ × 17 × 10 in.), stoneware with oxides, 1998.

Brickyard Angel by Dave Porter (USA). *The paper clay tubular inner support made all the difference, and fast drying was a big help. Green strength was fabulous.* Photograph courtesy of the Archie Bray Foundation.

RIGHT *Moving house* by Graham Hay (Australia). *The hot and dry Mediterranean climate in Perth, Western Australia is ideal for building in paper clay.*

Wall installation by Susan Wink (USA), unfired paper clay tiles.

Much experimentation and growth in this new but 'old' medium continues. As word gets out about the versatility of paper clays, expect to see many more wild juxtapositions and playful imaginative work, both fired and unfired.

Conclusion

Work with paper clay in all states of pliancy and/or density from soft to rigid, bone dry, even when partially fired at bisque. Build up or break down the form at will, as much or as little as necessary. No matter whether you choose to add or subtract, paper clay responds. It is up to you, the artist, to take advantage of what's appropriate for your style of work and vision.

The look of most paper clay after firing is for the most part impossible to distinguish from conventional clay. Lighter weight may be the only clue. All clays, when converted to paper clays, will shrink in drying and firing about the same as before. (Most paper clays shrink about 1% less than would be expected for the base clay without paper.) Paper clays never need to be aged either. Paper clays hardly ever need slow drying and even force-drying may be appropriate. With medium to high-pulp paper clay structures, thick can attach to thin. All the parts need not be of uniform width.

All in all, the technical and aesthetic possibilities of paper clay provide ceramicists with a most useful tool for creating their artistic visions in a way not possible that long ago.

Solid Vortex by Graham Hay.

Structure by Esben Klenman, (Denmark).

Appendix

Contents

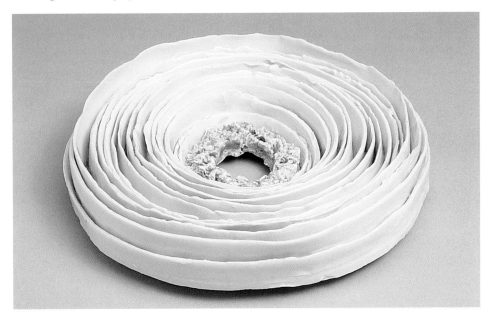

Close to the bone by Rosette Gault (USA). High-fired porcelain.

Normal firing schedule

Firing schedule time will vary due to:

1 Age and condition of your heating elements and fuel;
2 Dryness and thickness of sculpture or ware in kiln;
3 Amount of ware in kiln, size of kiln;
4 Moisture in atmosphere;
5 Ventilation in kiln.

Smoking from paper burning off will vary depending on how much paper clay is loaded in the kiln. Small amounts will hardly be noticed. Most commercial kiln venting equipment can handle larger jobs. Follow manufacturers' guidelines. There is normally much more smoke from a couple of sheets of crumpled newsprint than there is in paper clay itself.

	Room temperature	Boiling of water→steam	Paper burns	Smoking stops	Red heat	Finish Temp
Temperature	68°F ⇨⇨	212°F	451°F	⇨⇨	⇨⇨	⇨⇨ off
	20°C	100°C ⇨	232°C ⇨			
Time (elapsed since ignition)	Start	1–2 hours	3–4 hours	⇨⇨	6–8 hours	⇨⇨
Kiln controls	Low about 2 hours		Med about 2 hours		High	➡ off ➡ off
Ventilation (manual)	➡ ➡	Door/Lid Open		Door/Lid Closed	➡ ➡	➡ off ➡

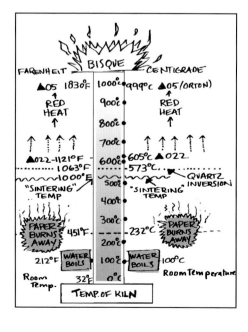

Firing fumes

The burn-off from wax resist resembles the burn-off of paper pulp. Both fumes have a recognisable smell, and occur near the same temperature very early on in the firing. Both periods last just an hour or two. The main difference is the paper burn-off can only occur once in paper clay and only during first firing. The fumes to worry about in firing clays are the ones you can't see or smell that any and all traditional clay and glaze materials release over the course of the fire. Those who neglect to ventilate their kilns deserve to suffer the consequences. No matter what you fire, fumes cannot be stopped.

Beware: avoid the 'fireproofed' so-called recycled newsprint pulp that is used for building material and insulation of human dwellings. Why? Toxic fumes from the fire retardent/pulp continue for hours and hours as they want to burn for as long as they possibly can!

Do not fire metals or plastics in pottery kilns without plentiful ventilation – fumes may be toxic. The results may also harm the kiln if they adhere to elements or kiln shelves!

Early stages of firing

Fahrenheit	toward porcelain and stoneware	Centigrade
2012°F	earthenware	1100°C
1830°F	Bisque red heat	1000°C
1652°F		900°C
1472°F	dull red heat	800°C
1121°F		700°C
1112°F	quartz	600°C
1063°F	inversion	573°C
1000°F	'sinter-set'	
932°F		500°C
752°F		400°C
572°F	paper	300°C
451°F	burns off	232°C
		200°C
212°F	water boils (vapour)	100°C
68°F	room temperature kiln ignition	20°C
32°F	water freezes (solid)	0°C

Recycling papers

Good paper sources	Paper description
Offices Schools	100% rag or linen writing papers *or* bond 25–50% rag (cotton)
Publishers Printers Letterpress Book pages	uncoated choose non-gloss book stock out of date brochures (most of the ink should be okay) use non-gloss (the gloss coat takes a long time to turn into pulp)
Artist studios	trimmings drawing papers cold press (easier) hot press
Copy centres Computers	cheap copy paper, ink and colours OK laser papers – long fibre*
Computers	lower grade laser and copy papers tractor feed multiple copy carbons
Newsprint	newsprint without plastic inks and glossy advertisements (colour can take more time)
Household	egg cartons
Miscellaneous	toilet rolls (will dissolve in cold water easily)
Avoid	vellums, coated paper, window envelopes, glossy junk mail*, staples, tape

* More difficult to pulp: requires top of the line pulp making tools and/or more mixing time – shorter fibres are easier.

To speed breakdown time:

1 Use plenty of hot water when mixing... the more the better.
2 Have papers shredded and sorted first. Test fire first (some newsprints/inks fire tan colours).

Tear or burst test of uncoated paper

Test of tearing	Cellulose fibres' relative length	Mixing time to pulp with hot water
Easy to tear	Short	1–5 minutes Easy 5–20 minutes
More difficult	Medium	10 minutes 2 hours (OK)
Difficult to tear	Long	Days or weeks Needs multiple straining and blunging

Wet over dry: a cup with paper thin walls. This was made from wet on dry assembly methods, using high quality porcelain casting slip.

Making or repairing using wet over dry

Cross section of 'wet' over 'dry'

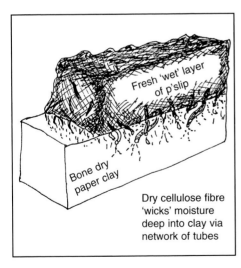

Fresh 'wet' layer of p'slip

Bone dry paper clay

Dry cellulose fibre 'wicks' moisture deep into clay via network of tubes

Path of a stress crack in paper clay

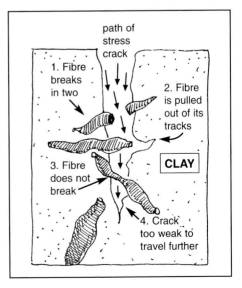

path of stress crack

1. Fibre breaks in two

2. Fibre is pulled out of its tracks

3. Fibre does not break

CLAY

4. Crack too weak to travel further

Recipe Adjustment Guidelines – Clay to Pulp
(Based on research by Rosette Gault)

Intended paper clay body application	Suitable classes of traditional clay slurry blends to start with	Suggested volume ratios of strained wet pulp to add *The more pulp you add the lighter fired weight and less plastic in the hands. The less you add the more claylike. The more clay like the more drying cracks you will have to patch, especially if wet on dry.*
Sculpture – table-top handbuilding	Stoneware, porcelain, terracotta, earthenware, casting slip, raku: without chamotte or sand that has been used to stabilise sculpture clays in the past.	Add 25-30% pulp to clay slip. The lower the amount of pulp, the less ease of wet on dry alteration and repair.
Sculpture (life-size)	Stoneware, porcelain, terracotta, earthenware, casting slip, raku: without chamotte, grog or sand that has been used to stabilise sculpture clays in the past.	Add 30-40% pulp to clay slip. I prefer about 33%.
Casting over plaster (ultra large scale)	Smooth Porcelain or low fire casting slip preferred, stoneware, earthenware terracotta ok if no rough texture.	Add 30 to 50% pulp to clay slip.
Casting slip over or in plaster (small scale)	Low fire casting slip or porcelain is typical.	Add 10–15 % pulp to clay slip. Short fibre is preferred if you expect the result to resemble casting slip instead of 'oatmeal' texture. Short fibre cellulose preparation is beyond the scope of this handbook.
Throwing on potters wheel (dishes, hand-held size objects)	Stoneware, earthenware, terra cotta, porcelain are typical.	Add 10-15 % pulp to clay slip. Short fibre cellulose is preferred so pots will be easier to trim at leather hard. Short fiber cellulose preparation is beyond the scope of this handbook.

Note: Do not blend different papers in the same mixing breakdown bucket, however it is ok to blend different types of pulp together. If you have a store-bought so called 'sculpture' body loaded to the max with chamotte, grog, sand or other non-clay texturizers and stabilisers, adding pulp to some of these can upset the ratio of plastic clay to non-clay and be crumbly before or after fire. To correct the ratio you must also blend in a good amount of plastic ball clay or china clay. Consider matching the volume of pulp to clay.

Marsh Report summary

This report, completed at the University of Kentucky, Louisville, Kentucky, in 1996 by Ginny Marsh, tested a variety of high-fire porcelain and stoneware paper clay recipes with various fillers.

Thin-walled paper clays can slump at high temperatures (beyond cone 6) just as much as the normal nonpaper clay does. However, paper pulp in combination with other fillers improved and corrected slump in many cases.

Fillers that were effective for high temperature paper clays:
1) 20% P-Grog can reduce deformation of a 20% (volume) pulp to zero, but 30% wood pulp was too much.
2) Kyanite/Feldspar, an invisible addition to stoneware, leaves grey spots on some porcelains. 1–2% of equal parts kyanite/feldpsar added to throwing body recipes will correct slumping. (Clays which had slumped 2 mm no longer slumped at all.) However, ratios are critical and all amounts must be specifically tested for the clay body in question. 'Thermal shock tests should be done to verify absorbtion of free silica' with these recipes too.

Over 2% kyanite in high-fire clays may defeat the purpose, and by 5% the paper clay will slump as much as the original recipe.

'The most effective means of reducing deformation of porcelains is to make them more refractory' according to Marsh. She suggests a cone 12 rated porcelain base for a slightly less than vitreous cone 9 paper clay result.

Fillers that were not effective in Marsh tests:
1) Molochite: 10% 'raised blemishes in porcelains and caused glazes to craze so I abandoned it'.
2) Alumina: 5% produced no effect on slumping.
3) Calcined EPK reduced deformation but kaolin was better.

Marsh also tested wood fibre pulp compared to cotton linters. She preferred the wood fibre pulp. If you are making substitutions of cotton to wood pulp equivalent amounts would be as follows. 'This chart makes it clear how much cellulose is added when working with cotton linter pulp' (cotton: 96% cellulose, wood pulp: about 50% cellulose).

Percent by volume in recipe

Cotton linter	Wood fibre
5%	9.6%
8%	15.4%
10%	19.2%
15%	28.8%
20%	38.4%
25%	48.0%
30%	57.6%

More detailed testing is currently in progress on high-fire stonewares and porcelains by Marsh and others. In sum, the amount and type of paper pulp used does affect the outcome. Marsh concludes that less than 20% by volume cotton linter is recommended for high-fire porcelain work.

Juvonen Report

Published in 8th CIMTEC World Ceramics Congress, Florence, Italy, June 1994: by Leena Juvonen, University of Art and Design UIAH , Helsinki, Finland.

This report tested eight different types of pulp with the same clay base at various firing temperatures ranging from 1100°–1250°C (2012°–2282°F). Green strength, porosity, shrinkage and fired strength were measured from the uniform test bar samples. She tested by weight, 2%, 10% and 20% proportions of pulp to clay.

Juvonen's work confirmed Kingery's earlier observation of the improved green strength of all the tests. She further went on to determine that:
1) The type of pulp used will affect the green strength, with the shredded paper and certain wood pulp being the stronger of the pulps at greenware. (The base clay alone measured 1.0, the strongest of the 2% pulp group being 1.8, and the strongest of the 10% pulp group measured 2.1, near to or beyond double the green strength of the base overall.)
2) Any amount of pulp beyond 2% (calculated by weight percentage) would cause dramatic loss of fired strength compared to the base clay. And at 2% by weight, the loss of fired strength was in the range of 18–40% depending on the fibre she tested. At 20% by weight the loss was extreme: 75%–90%.

(Volume calculations, by my research, suggest that 2% by weight is approximately 20–40% by volume. So, Juvonen confirms that too much pulp will surely cause some reduction in strength unless certain adjustments are made to the parent clay. The adjustments suggested in the Marsh report could be a point of departure for further research.)

Juvonen conducted a parallel practical and aesthetic study of accomplishing very thin, very large bow forms which could be fired intact. She concludes that the increased green strength of paper clay made transporting these thin delicate forms from the mould to the kiln possible. She found she could begin firing even when the object was still wet. Also, one-fire glazing, eliminating the bisque fire, was very successful.

A daring work in progress by Jiri Lonsky (Czech Republic/USA). Using p'clay, greenware can be more easily transported to the kiln without fear of collapse, P'clay allows for more imagination and freedom with clay forms.

Displacement scales compared

Adapted from Kingery Test, University of Arizona, 1993.

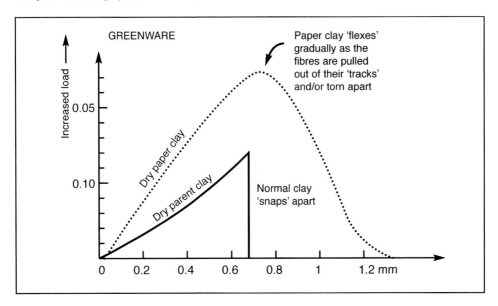

GREENWARE

Increased load →

0.05

0.10

Dry paper clay

Dry parent clay

Paper clay 'flexes' gradually as the fibres are pulled out of their 'tracks' and/or torn apart

Normal clay 'snaps' apart

0   0.2   0.4   0.6   0.8   1   1.2 mm

Forming Methods, Surfaces and Colours

Form over chickenwire by Gudrun Klix (Australia), 'I pressed low-pulp p'clay into a chickenwire "frame" and fired them together – cracks appeared due to low-pulp but I think they go with the piece'.

Paper clay: methods summary

Condition of clay		Additive methods	Subtractive methods	Surface
oatmeal consistency P'slip	adhesive	smear or pour to build up thickness or texture, some versions can be poured over clay in plaster moulds	—	smear or brush thick or thin
wedged plastic modelling	coils pinch pugs	press-moulds assemble	carve and model	screen print, stamps imprinting
leathersoft	drapes and soft pliant sheets, cut tiles	may assemble with p'slip	carve out with care, use needle or stick to cut, or scissors if thin	rib burnish imprint textures screen print
leatherhard	stiff to handle, slab construction	score (option) and use p'slip assemble	carve with sharp tool drill on, use needle or stick	burnish imprint texture
Work on bone dry	**assembly, slab box constructions**	**repair of cracks, wet with water, score with p'slip and paper clay on both ends and press together**	**water wet first – usually makes carving easier, can snap and score, break apart, saw on, or drill into**	**screen print or texture or coloured slip or glaze application**
'Sinter set fired' 540°C/1004°F		**may be able to join greenware or to bisque of paper clay**	**carves into powder**	**may be able to add slip, glaze or textures**
Bisque 1000°C/1832°F		**may be able to repair cracks, and/or build directly over wet bisque with p' slip and paper clay and rebisque again**	**manual blade carving usually not possible except with some porcelains. May be possible to carve with rotary power tool like a Dremel tool**	**glazes and stains may be applied**
At maturity temperature of clay				refire and reglaze matt surfaces only

Over-fired forms will slump, and ultimately liquefy, with both clay and p'clay.

Bold typeface shows expanded sculptural freedom possible with paper clays.

Template shapes for common forms

Cutout flat shape	Folds to freestanding form
Cone 1	2
Cone 1	2
'Pants' legs 1	2 ▶ ▶ 3
Torso top; 'vest' 1	2 ▶
Torso top; 'shirt with shoulders' 1	2
4 legged form 1	2 3

A ceramicist's colour palette: a multi-purpose system

The following system is a versatile means of making a reliable colour palette that is compatible with both paper clay and conventional clay. The concept is simple: instead of making glaze colour recipes out of raw materials, mix prepared ingredients instead. Commercial glazes and slips do not generate airborne dust in your studio and they do not require a scale. The following is a system for making your own all-temperature underglazes or coloured slips. These slips may perform in a manner similar to terra sigillatas at high-fire.

Part I Set up and selection of a slip base

A) Test clay and (commercial) glaze compatibility

1) Select a clay you like to work with. I prefer white firing clays because colours show up better on these and there is a greater range of choice of surface colour. Also select or prepare a (casting) slip similar to the clay body you use. Test fire if necessary.

2) Choose an all-purpose, low-fire transparent clear glaze that is compatible with the clay body you have, i.e. it does not craze or crackle. Test fire to the desired temperature as many different brands of glazes over stripes (on bisque) of colour stain, especially pinks, maroons, purples, blues, yellows and browns, as these are prone to changes. (Check the label to make sure that the material is lead-free.) Choose the brand you like that 'fits' your clay and colour stain best. (Note: most commercial low-fire glazes can also be fired at a high temperature if applied super thin.)

B) Make a line blend of clay and glaze (optional)

To find the surface melt you like at the temperature you fire – use six or more mixing containers and mark them A, B, C, D... etc. With a cup, measure out into each container as follows in the table.

Line blending examples Recipes A–G. Each one has different volume proportions giving a different surface 'melt' of slip and glaze.

Test recipe	A	B	C	D	E	F	G
Liquid Clear glaze (parts by volume)	6	5	4	3	2	1	0
Liquid Casting slip (parts by volume)	0	1	2	3	4	5	6
Result of surface appearance	All glaze gloss surface	5/1	2/1	equal parts	1/2	5/1	All slip matt surface
Total parts	6	6	6	6	6	6	6

Select the preferred surface from these tests for your base – matt surface, like recipe E or F, will likely be a more versatile all-purpose base.

Volume measure the ratios using a consistent unit – such as a tablespoon or cup.

Paint a few stripes, thick and thin, of each test – A, B, C, etc. – on a test tile and identify each. Fire to bisque, then refire to desired final temperature. Observe results.

You should notice melting as follows in the line blend below:

Sample line blend							G = glaze
(To find a good base slip that is compatible with your clay.)							S = slip
Ingredients	**Test A**	**Test B**	**Test C**	**Test D**	**Test E**	**Test F**	**Test G**
Volume units	G6/S0	G5/S1	G4/S2	G3/S3	G2/S4	G1/S5	G0/S6
Fired Result	shiny ➡	shiny ➡		semi ➡	matt ➡		very
Surface	clear	matt		matt			matt
Appearance	gloss						

C) Choose a base mixture from your line blend above

Make a batch of base slip out of clay slip and glaze in proportions you like for the surface you want to have. For matt surface at bisque: slip to glaze 90s/10g or 80s/20g – a higher proportion of glaze for a more glazelike look. Use the same size cup, a ruler or your eye to measure volumes in a larger container. Mix enough base to fill the containers of each colour you plan to have in your palette, then add stains.

Layout of slips for colour palette development. Numbered containers of concentrate correspond to the list of colours on p.128. I use the same base from line blending tests for all the colours. These can be watered down for use as a transluscent wash, or used thick as an opaque cover.

Part 2 Mixing some base colours

A) Gather supplies
Make up a liquid base slip as described in Part 1, and gather and label (with indelible ink on cloth adhesive tape) enough lidded containers for separate colours.

B) Stir in colours
Wear gloves and mask. Put approximately ½–¾ cup (100–200 ml) of powder stain in a cup. With water, stir to a paste or thick cream. Try to remove most of the lumps at this stage. Then add the wet stain colour concentrate to the container (one cup) of liquid base slip. When you see that the base is saturated and intense with colour, *stop*. The amount of stain needed will vary depending on the stain you have and how much base you started with. Keep a record of how much stain you have used for each colour. Strain the mix three times to get all the lumps out. Store the concentrate in an airtight container. Use the colour like a slip or underglaze with brushes, sponges, etc. Thin with water or slip as necessary.

Colour key for palette (Gault name and number)	Mason Stain added to the base mixture (suggestion only)	Note oxide/stain you use or substitute (mix in base)	Note amount of stain used
Yellow # 1	6440		
Orange-Yellow #2	6464		
Pink #3	6020		
Maroon #4	6381		
Lavender #5	6319		
Dark Green #6	6468		
Teal #7	6266		
Light Green #8	6242		
Sky Blue #9	6379		
Royal Blue #10	6300		
Med. Blue #11	6371		
Blue #12	6396		
Black #13	6600		
Dark Brown # 14	6134		
Light Brown # 15			
Grape # 16	6338		

Part 3 Applying coloured slips and engobes to surfaces

Whether for sculpture or pottery, your choice of colour and application will distinguish your work from that of others. As in house paint, there are three basic surface categories – matt (no gloss), semi-gloss (satin matt) and gloss – to choose and interweave. Substitutions and variations should be encouraged. Experiment and test!

Level 1 Slip
Build up layers and layers of thick and thin coloured slips. Fire to bisque in-between coats if setting the colour is desired or correction of uneven brush-work is needed. My Level 1 colours are in a base that fires open with a porous

High texture is brushed on in successive layers using deflocculated slip and glaze over a dry paper clay form. *Photographs by Sue Hungerford.*

surface (claylike) at bisque. I can even do some colour changes if needed at bisque. Also, I can do washes, and highlighting at bisque.

Best of all, these slips can be applied directly on the wet, leather, leatherhard or greenware, and they can be carved over, scratched through, and/or built up thick into textured surfaces. All manner of corrections are possible before the first firing.

Skill and variety of application is in the master's hand. The more colours to mix, the more variations. Practise. The number of textures possible is infinite!

Level 2 Semi-matt glaze
(For advanced work only) Make another set of colours by substituting a transparent satin matt glaze for the base. The surface may be waxy; it can't be changed at bisque, but it usually deepens colours and surfaces. Highlights and many more colour choice and combinations are also possible.

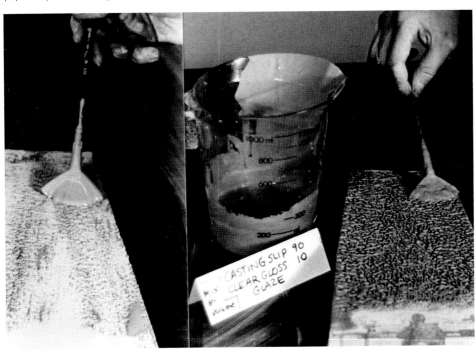

Level 3 Final glaze

A transparent gloss glaze will seal the surface and the colours cannot then be changed. A gloss coat is necessary for dinnerware. Apply low-fire glazes as directed on the label for low firings.

1. TOP Sponge colours of thinned 'slip' onto dry or wet paper clay surface. Rub off any excess.
2. BELOW; LEFT Brush thickened colour of choice (black layer shown) over the top of the colour to give texture and depth.
3. BELOW; RIGHT Carve off the colour in crisp perfect lines back to the white clay. If you don't like the results you can always put more colour over it or sponge it off.

Cross section of a 'sandwich' of clay, slips and glaze.

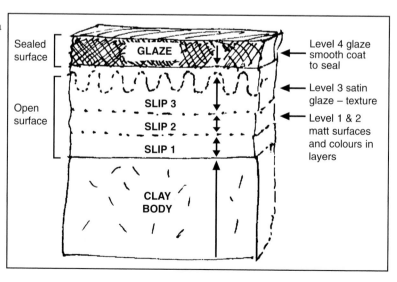

Additions to Clays

Particle sizes compared

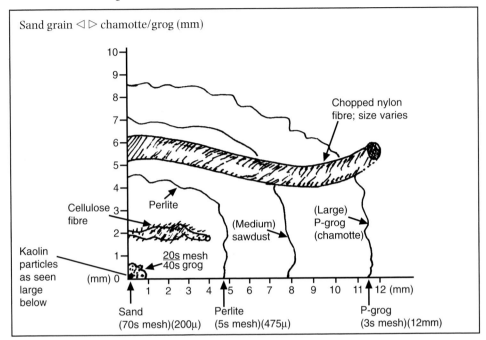

Sand grain ◁ ▷ chamotte/grog (mm)

Chopped nylon fibre; size varies

Cellulose fibre

Perlite

(Medium) sawdust

(Large) P-grog (chamotte)

Kaolin particles as seen large below

20s mesh 40s grog

Sand (70s mesh)(200μ)

Perlite (5s mesh)(475μ)

P-grog (3s mesh)(12mm)

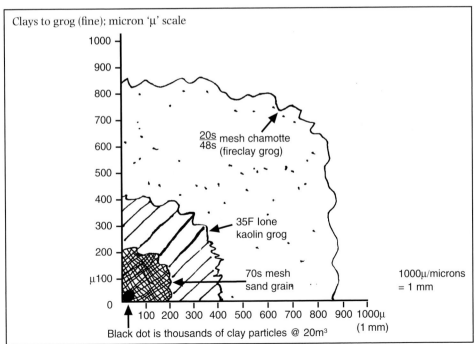

Clays to grog (fine); micron 'μ' scale

20s/48s mesh chamotte (fireclay grog)

35F lone kaolin grog

70s mesh sand grain

1000μ/microns = 1 mm

Black dot is thousands of clay particles @ 20m³

(1 mm)

Particle size comparison of common clay additives

US Mesh Tyler scale (openings/sq. in. in sieve)	Metric 'mm' size (size of each opening in sieve)	Examples
1s mesh	26.5 mm	gravel
2.5s mesh	8.0 mm	P-grog-chamotte (maximum)
3s mesh	6.7 mm	Sawdust – size varies
5s mesh	4.0 mm	perlite (4s mesh max)
8s mesh	2.3 6 mm	small cellulose fibres
20s mesh	850 µ	coarse grog/chamotte
3 5s mesh	425 µ	grogs/chamottes, large kyanite
42s mesh	355 µ	fine grog or chamotte
65s mesh	212 µ	very fine grain sand
200s mesh	75 µ	glazes
325s mesh	45 µ	glazes – small kyanites
400s mesh	36 µ	small fireclay particle sizes
–	10 µ–0.2µ	average size range for clay particles: kaolins, ball and china clays
–	1µ = 0.001mm	small bacteria
–	0.1 µ	large colloidal particles – bentonites
–	0.01 µ	large molecule

Data compiled from W.S.Tyler Inc. Chart, Parmelee, Whitney, Cardew and Company, clay manufacturers.

Additive fillers – an alternative to grog, perlite (fires white) and vermiculite (fires tan–brown) can be used (see recipes on p.134). Chamotte is good for sculpture (see p.51) as it is much lighter than grog after firing.

Cellulose and nylon compared

Natural cellulose fibre

(may include cotton, flax, linen, hard and soft wood sources)

- Hollow-irregular, tapered tube shape, stretches
- Water absorbent interior of tube, shrinks dry and swells up wet, flexible and resilient to bending, stretching and flattening
- Can bounce back to original tube shape after stress
- Natural source
- Exterior is rough, not smooth
- Smaller length, in clay bodies barely visible.

Nylon or manufactured fibre

- Extruded, not hollow, cylinder shape with uniform diameter, stretches
- Exterior is smooth
- Much longer length, but can be ordered to variety of sizes
- Does not wick water
- Does not absorb water
- Long shelf life

Clay memory

1. A soft slab for a large tile on plaster. In the beginning... Uniform particles of undisturbed paper clay or paper slip.

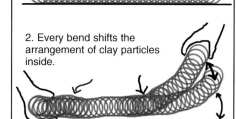

2. Every bend shifts the arrangement of clay particles inside.

3. The uneven alignment of particles is temporarily hidden, and is still there even after rollers are used.

4. As the water evaporates the clay tries to return to the previous shape.

Understanding this aspect of clay, that it has a 'memory', will help you during making and firing.

Book by Nancy Selvin (USA).

Recipes

Test fire all of these with your local materials first. I cannot be responsible for non-standard materials, events and results that are clearly beyond my control. Also, the high speciality recipes given here are not equivalent to standard Paperclay or Paperslip licensed product. I use these for large-scale outdoor/indoor sculpture.

'Rosetta Stone' earthenware paper clay for sculpture - Cone 04–4

This was my 'high-fire, low-fire' high pulp all-purpose any kiln, any time sculpture clay for years.

Two (2) medium buckets prepared 'earthenware' base (rated cone 04–05) low-fire casting slip.
One medium bucket of pulp, plus or minus handfuls (disperse paper from 8–12 rolls of bargain toilet tissue, the equivalent to maybe eight bulkier rolls of standard brand).

Texture and Touch

Texture Before Fire: Smooth, puttylike. Takes underglazes, slip, engobe, stains etc.
Bone Dry: Absorbs water when dipped. Takes underglaze, slip, engobe, stains, glaze etc.
Thin walls soften a bit when soaked a while. Slakes down overnight or sooner.
Sinter Fired: Carves like frozen butter.
Texture-After-Fire: Smooth and white, the higher it is fired the more dense and hard it gets after cone 4.
Biscuit Fired (cone 4-6): Hard as rock. Resembles white stoneware. Resists water but is not 100% watertight. OK outdoors in freeze and thaw too – glazed and not glazed.

Substitutions/Adaptions

Raku: Good anytime – bisque high (04 or more) first. When you know your kiln, the fuel, the tools and tongs, how the shapes heat up and where to place them, bone dry single fire works.
China 'Paints' Gold/ Silver/ Metallic/ Mother of Pearl/ Lustre/ Decal Fires: Most want just cone 032. Best to apply on top of already fired gloss glazes.
Base Clay Options: If you substitute an iron bearing red terracotta blended clay as base for the earthenware, this will fire red to brown when the recommended lower temperature of 05–4 is followed.

Nina Holes's recipe (from 1996 Sculpture Fired Event, Sonoma State College, California)

	(by volume)
soft scrap clay (stoneware)	1
pulp (toilet tissue)	0.75
water	0.5
fireclay	0.75

Dean Goss (USA)
Trowelable over metals

In addition to those mentioned in the Paper Clay Mixture #2 cone 04, 1050°C (1922°F). Test first.

Soda Spar	347
EPK Kaolin	217
Flint (Silica)	173
Soda Ash	53
Whiting ($CaCO_3$)	43
OM 4 Ball clay	43
Ferro Frit 3124	70
Sodium Bicarbonate	52
Cotton Linter	70
Total	1025

'Porcelain Pearl' paper clay for sculpture

Thin areas go translucent at cone 8. Dare to fire to cone 10 *only* if walls are thick (and other factors mentioned in text) indicate structure is stable and well-built. For mixing batches in the studio, avoid or minimise airborne dust clouds by starting with buckets of prepared liquid casting/pouring slip rather than large bags of dry blend powdered clay.

Two (2) medium buckets prepared 'porcelain' (cone 10) high-fire casting slip one medium bucket of pulp plus or minus handfuls (disperse paper from 8–12 rolls of 'bargain' toilet tissue equivalent to maybe eight bulkier rolls of standard).

Texture and Touch
Texture Before Fire: Chunky peanut butter – very short when moist. Takes under-glaze, slip, engobe, stains and glaze etc.
Bone Dry: Absorbs water when dipped. Thin walls soften a bit when soaked for a short time. Slakes down overnight or sooner. Takes underglaze, slip, engobe, stains and glaze etc.
Texture After Fire: Surface openings like a utility sponge, irregular granulated pocks, lightweight, strong if fired to just the right melt.
Sinter Fired: Carves like frozen butter, dense and still easy to handle.
Biscuit Fired: Low (cone 8), may be friable so handle with extreme care. Carves more like a dry cosmetic grade sponge. Higher: Cone (03) is less friable, OK to carve but not as nice as sinter. Does not slake down.
High Fire: Cone 8–10 hard as rock. If walls thin go to cone 8 and play it safe. Serious power tools needed to alter surface.

Substitutions/Adaptions
Base Clay Substitution: If you substitute stoneware throwing clay as base for the porcelain – fires tan to brown.
Raku: Good anytime – bisque high (03 or more) first. When you know your kiln, the fuel, the tools and tongs, how the shapes heat up and where to place them, bone dry single firing is fine.
China 'Paints' / Gold / Silver / Metallic / Mother of Pearl / Lustre / Decal Fires: Most need cone 032. Best to apply on top of already fired gloss glazes.

'Ruff-Rock-Gruff-Rock'
Porcelain sculpture cone 8–10
Two (2) medium buckets prepared 'porcelain' (cone 10) high fire casting slip $^1/_2$ medium bucket of pulp – plus or minus handfuls (disperse paper from 8–12 rolls of 'bargain' toilet tissue equivalent to maybe eight bulkier rolls of standard). $^1/_2$ medium bucket granular perlite – plus or minus handfuls.

Texture and Touch
Texture Before Fire: Chunky peanut butter, very short when moist. Takes underglaze, slip, engobe, stains and glaze.
Bone Dry: Absorbs water when dipped or sprayed. Softens then slakes when soaked over time. Takes underglaze, slip engobe, stains and glaze etc.

Using a chisel to carve down the bone hard – unfired – 'Ruff Rock' porcelain sculpture paper clay with the Perlite texture.

Texture After Fire: Surface openings like a utility sponge, irregular granulated pocks, lightweight and strong if fired just to the right melt.

Sinter Fired: Carves like frozen chunky peanut butter.

Biscuit Fired: Low (cone 8): May be friable, (OK to carve but not as nice as sinter). Takes underglaze, slip, engobe, stains, glaze etc.

High Fire: Cone 8–9 hard as rock. Serious power tools needed. Gloss glaze and clay resist moisture.

Substitutions/Adaptions

Base Clay Substitution: If you substitute stoneware throwing clay as base for the porcelain – fires tan to brown.

Raku: Good anytime – bisque high (03 or more) first. When you know your kiln, the fuel the tools and tongs, how the shapes heat up, and where to place them, bone dry single fire is fine.

China 'Paints' Gold / Silver / Metallic / Mother of Pearl / Lustre / Decal Fires: Most need cone 032. Best to apply on top of already fired gloss glazes.

Earthenware Paper Clay (from University of Delaware).

Bentonite	2 lb
Ball clay OM4	10 lb
Saggar XX (a brick fireclay)	9 lb
Gold Art (a terracotta clay)	27 lb
Custer Spar	7 lb
Wollastonite	5 lb
kyanite	34 lb (up to 55 lb)
pulp (high rag)	15% (by volume)
(Add more pulp as needed.)	

Lifelight by Linda Stanier, 46 × 66 × 25.5 cm (18 × 26 × 10 in.). Multi-fired ceramic and paper clay.

Make your own plaster work surface

To make your own plaster slab is not too difficult and it will have many uses in the studio, not just for paper clay work.

Advance preparation

Tools and material
Get two 5 gallon buckets: one for measuring the water and one for measuring the plaster. I mark the right level of the weighed volume on the side of each bucket with indelible black, so it's easy to remeasure new batches consistently by volume thereafter.

I spray the inside of the empty water bucket with a light film coat of silicon spray such as WD40 and wipe the surface so that a thin film remains. Measure the water required in a separate bucket. Water temperature is important. The water should be *lukewarm*. If too hot, the plaster sets too quickly. If the water is too cold, then the plaster sets too slowly.

Professionals also make sure the plaster they use is as fresh and dry as possible, ideally less than six months old. Immediately double plastic wrap or bag the plaster as soon as it arrives in the studio and keep it away from moisture, wet or damp cement floors and the like. Check the contents of the bag for any granulated lumps which result from moisture. Exchange the bag for fresh immediately if necessary.

Stir the dry powdered plaster in the bucket by hand to aerate the plaster and fluff it up. You will notice the plaster change texture as it is stirred. Now it is ready.

Making cottles
Cottles can range from cookie sheets/baking trays or cafeteria trays to more elaborate box forms. For multiple small-scale portable light duty slabs, such as those that might be used in classroom situations or in series work, something like cafeteria trays or 21.5 x 35.5 cm ($8\frac{1}{2}$ x 14 in.) metal baking trays (the ones without a graphic texture imprinted on the metal) will do. These should be set out on a level surface before pouring begins. Plaster slabs poured into smaller trays are less bulky and can be stored more easily.

For professional use, I recommend making a set of four adjustable cottle walls which you will clamp together to the precise dimension of slab you require. These are best made of linoleum, formica or similarly treated shelving, cut to the very largest possible size you would use. These also can be reused and reassembled again and again whenever you have to make a plaster mould. These result in a perfect surface to the walls of your plaster mould which is easy to clean.

A more casual approach to this is to sculpt the walls out of scrap clay. The clay wall method of cottle making is usually a one-time, one-of-a-kind project.

Find a smooth seamless surface like linoleum, formica or glass large enough for the bottom of the cottle. This surface will be ultimately the top of the finished slab – the work surface. I consider the maximum width of my kiln when planning the dimension of this slab. With a level, I make sure that the cottle base is secure and true. (Otherwise the plaster will settle unevenly in the cottle, and your slab will be uneven.)

At this point, I assemble or build the walls. I also putty in the cracks with a thin coil of fresh clay, so that the whole frame will not leak liquid plaster during the pour.

If a mould release agent is used, be absolutely sure the 'soap' has dried out completely on the surface before pouring begins. Sponge or brush on three very thin coats, letting each *dry* in between

scrapes and chips off easily, thus possibly contaminating the clay. Too much plaster with the water and the resulting slab is tough and impenetrable, slower at absorbing water than it could be, which is a waste of good plaster.

When the cottle is ready, sprinkle plaster into the water, handful by handful from above without agitating the bucket. Let the whole mix stand still, unagitated for several minutes. Then with rotary blender disc or with hands, agitate and stir the mix for four minutes, being careful not to whip in excess air which could cause bubbles later. With experience you can tell just when the plaster is starting to change viscosity. The ideal time to pour is just at first notice of this change while the plaster is viscous.

Pour plaster over the edge of the cottle so a smooth puddle of liquid rolls over the flat surface of the cottle like a wave of incoming tide. Move the bucket as you pour. If you simply empty the bucket in one place, the plaster will have a different density at that one place, and thus will not absorb as much water. This can be a cause of uneven castings in the future.

I pour excess plaster into the extra smaller forms or cottles. Gently tap or agitate the tabletop with a hammer, about six times on each side to release stray air bubbles that might be stuck on the bottom of the flat surface. Let the plaster set in the bucket only if the bucket was pretreated with silicon such as WD40. When the plaster hardens, it won't stick to the sides of the pretreated bucket and the broken debris is disposed of easily. If I haven't pretreated the bucket, I empty as much plaster out as possible in the garbage bin (dustbin), then fill the bucket full with fresh water immediately before the plaster has hard-

and especially before your pour. I recommend using the right concentration of mould release soap, rather than vaseline which may clog the absorbent pores of your plaster. Mould release soaps are usually not required for water-resistant smooth surfaces such as glass or metal. Pliant or leatherhard clay does not need it either. Only really absorbent surfaces, like wood, bisque or other plaster will need soaping.

Before the pour I usually make a mark for the right level of plaster with a bit of masking tape tacked on the inside of the cottle. This way I don't make the slab too thin or too thick.

Plaster mixing and pouring process

Professionals use the recipes and measure and weigh out the water. This way they get the exact best possible water absorbency and strength out of their plaster. The result is repeatable, consistent and reliable. Too little plaster with the water and the slab is so soft that it

RIGHT *Rollup* by Rosette Gault (USA). Paper clay with vermiculite added, fires brown as can be seen.

ened. Rinse off the sides with a rag or sponge and stir. Dispose of diluted plaster water, but not down the sink. Flush the drain with fresh water immediately.

After the pour, caring for plaster moulds

If you notice a pool of water formed on top of your setting plaster, do not worry. The water temperature, ratio of water to plaster and the timing of the pour are among the causes for this. Sponge up what you can from the top and wait for evaporation.

As plaster hardens (10–30 minutes or so), the set will feel hot to the touch. Then you can gently release the clamps on the cottle and free up the walls. If you release the cottle too soon, the plaster might crumble. I clean up everything with a sponge as I go. The plaster is still what I would describe as semi-hard, very easily scraped or carved at this stage, and fragile too. With a knife I can scrape or carve the rough edges of the new slab and make the whole slab nice and smooth.

The slab looks right at this point but it is too wet to absorb water and will feel damp too. Let the entire slab dry out propped up (so that air can reach both sides) in a dry warm room for maybe two weeks. To speed this process, moving air is the best strategy. Place a rotating fan nearby and you will shorten the drying process to days. I do not advise putting slabs in kilns to dry/bake them with radiant heat. Force-dried slabs of plaster resaturate with water much too easily, and tend to crumble and scratch. If you've gone to the trouble of making a proper slab you will use for years, why risk failure from haste at the very end of the process?

Over years of use, plaster will break down and water absorption will diminish. To get the maximum service life possible, keep the following ideas in mind.

- Never let the mould get too hot
- Temperatures over 54°C (130°F) may cause the calcium in plaster to crumble into a powder. Room temperature storage is best
- Avoid freezing
- Ventilate your slabs. I store my slabs supported on several sticks or slats of wood. This way, air reaches all sides to dry the slab in-between use and moisture can evaporate from below the slab. A plaster slab is like a giant stone sponge
- Moulds can be wiped off easily with a sponge. Keep plaster clean to avoid clogging the microscopic pores which will affect the rate of water absorbency
- Avoid anything oily, soapy or waxy on the surfaces. Finally, use only plastic or wood tools (gently) on the surface as metal tools can scratch the surface.

Bibliography

Magazines

The following journals contain articles on paper clay by the author and others. All sources mentioned published since 1992.

In English:
Artist's Newsletter (UK)
a-n The Artists Information Company
First Floor, 7 – 15 Pink Lane
Newcastle Upon Tyne, NE1 5DW

Ceramics Monthly (USA)
The American Ceramic Society, P.O. Box 6136, Westerville, OH 43086-6136
www.ceramicsmonthly.org

Ceramic Review (UK)
25 Foubert's Place, London, W1F 7QF
www.ceramicreview.com

Ceramics, Art and Perception (Australia)
120 Glenmore Road Paddington, Sydney, NSW 2021
www.ceramicart.com.au

Pottery in Australia (Australia)
PO Box 105, Erskineville, NSW 2043
www.australianceramics.com

New Zealand Potter (New Zealand)
PO Box 881, Auckland

NCECA Journal 1993 (USA)
77 Erie Village Square, Suite 280
Erie, Colorado 80516-6996

Form and Function (Finland)
Erottajankatu I5-17 A, 00130 Helsinki

Other languages:

Revista Ceramica (Madrid, Spain)
La Revue de la Ceramique (France)
Keramik Magazin and *Neue Keramik* (Germany)
Dansk Kunst Handvaerk (Denmark)
Stook (Netherlands)

Books

Gault, Rosette, *Paper Clay for Ceramic Sculptors*, Clear Light, Seattle, 1993, (Second Edition 1996)

Hopper, Robin, and Rhodes, Daniel, *Clay and Glazes for the Potter*, Krause Publications, USA/A & C Black, London, Third edition 2000

Lane, Peter, *Contemporary Porcelain – Materials, Techniques and Expressions*, A & C Black, London/Chilton Book Company, Philadelphia/ Craftsman House, Australia, 1995

Peterson, Susan, *The Craft and Art of Clay*, Prentice Hall, Revised edition, 1995

Scott, Paul, *Ceramics and Print*, A& C Black, London, 1994

BELOW *Voyage* by Rosette Gault (USA), silk screened, glazed and altered earthenware, 38 × 5 × 10 cm (15 × 2 × 4 in.).

List of Suppliers

For most recent listings:
Website: wwwpaperclayart.com

In UK

Paper Clay Products
Blacksmith Shop
Tontrilas
Hereford, HR2 OBB
Tel: 01981-240427
Fax: 01981-240953

TCAS (Metrosales)
Unit 3, 46 Mill Place
Kingston upon Thames, KT12 2RL
Tel: 0208-546-1108
Fax: 0208-546-9683

In USA/Canada

The trade marks P'Clay® and/or P'Slip® are owned by New Century Arts. Commercially prepared paper clay products with these trademarks meet the highest possible quality control standards of the author.

Patent is pending on commercial uses of some of the mixing processes mentioned in part in this book. License is granted to individual artists to prepare paper clays for original works of art however. US Patent No. 5,72 6,111 was issued.

For the distributor or manufacturer nearest you, or for licensing information, please contact: New Century Arts, PO Box 9060, Seattle, WA 98109, USA.

If your local supplier does not yet carry what you need, the following vendors may be able to help:

Axner Pottery Supply
Oviedo-Orlando, Florida, USA
Tel: 1-800-843-7057
Fax: 407-365-5573
P'Clay® and P'Slip®: ready-made and custom order licensed manufacturer

Clay Art Centre
2636 Pioneer Way E.
Tacoma, WA 98404
Tel: 1-800-952-8030
P'Clay® and P'Slip®: ready-made and custom order licensed manufacturer

East Bay Clay
200 South First Street
Richmond, CA 94804
Tel: 510-233-1800

IMCO (Industrial Minerals)
Sacramento, CA
Tel: 916-383-2811

Mile Hi Ceramics
77 Lipan, Denver, Colorado
CO 80223-1580
Tel: (303) 825-4570/1-800-456-0163
www.milehiceramics.com

Tuckers Pottery Supply
15 West Pearce Street, Unit 7
Richmond Hill (near Toronto),
Ontario, L4B 1H6 Canada
Tel: 905-889-7705, 1-800-304-6185
Fax: 905-889-7707
P'Clay® and P'Slip® ready-made and custom order

Peter Pugger Manufacturing
12501 Orr Springs Road
Ukiah, CA 95482
Tel: 707-463-1333

*Other USA sources of paper clay products, pulp,
or books as at time of writing include:*

A.R.T. Studio Clay Company
9320 Michigan Avenue, Sturtevant,
WI 53177-2425
Tel: (262) 884-4278
www.artclay.com

Continental Clay Company
1101 Stintson Blvd, N.E. Minneapolis,
Minnesota, MN 55413
Tel: (800) 432-2529
www.continentalclay.com

The Potters Shop
31 Thorpe Road, Needham, Massachusetts
MA 02194
Tel: (781) 449-7687

Trinity Ceramic Supplies
9016 Diplomacy Row, Dallas, Texas
TX 75247
Tel: 214-631-0540
Fax 214-637-6463

In Australia

Artisan Craft Books
159 Gertrude St, Fitzroy, Victoria 3065
Tel: (03) 9416 4805
Fax: (03) 9416 4806

Clayworks Australia Pty Ltd
6 Johnston Court, Dandenong,
Victoria 3175
Tel: (03) 791-6749
Fax: (03) 792-4476

Claycraft Supplies Pty Ltd
29 O'Connell Terrace, Bowen Hills,
Queensland 4006
Tel: (07) 3854 1515

The Pugmill Pty Ltd
Shop 13, 42 New St, Ringwood,
Victoria 3134
Tel: (03) 9870-7533
Fax: (03) 9870-7033

For Raw Materials:
Cook Industrial Minerals Pty Ltd
Cutler Road
Jandakot, West Australia 6164
Tel: (08) 941 7111

Cretaceous Light, by Angela Mellor,
from bone china p'slip.

Index